Ready to Serve

*A training course
preparing church members
for active ministry*

Lance Pierson

based on Core Year,
the Adult Training Programme
at All Souls' Church, Langham Place

originally devised by Andrew Cornes

BIBLE SOCIETY

BRITISH AND FOREIGN BIBLE SOCIETY
Stonehill Green, Westlea, Swindon SN5 7DG, England

A catalogue record for this book is available from the British Library
ISBN 05640 8705 X

Printed in Great Britain by Swindon Press Ltd

Cover design by Litchfield Morris, Gloucester

Bible Societies exist to provide resources for Bible distribution and use. The British and Foreign Bible Society (BFBS) is a member of the United Bible Societies, an international partnership working in over 180 countries. Their common aim is to reach all people with the Bible, or some part of it, in a language they can understand and at a price they can afford. Parts of the Bible have now been translated into over 2,000 languages. Bible Societies aim to help every church at every point where it uses the Bible. You are invited to share in this work by your prayers and gifts. The Bible Society in your country will be very happy to provide details of its activity.

Contents

SERIES 3: FINDING THE JOB GOD WANTS ME TO DO IN MY CHURCH

Acknowledgements

The author wishes to thank the following for their unstinting, indispensable help in preparing this course for publication:

Anne Ballard, Katherine Cornes, Yvonne Kane and Yasmin Muttiah for expertise and elbow-grease as assistants to the author – they worked so hard that they are really co-authors; Sue Radford, Gillian Nicholls, Lis Scott, Chris Payne, Marie Reynolds and Henrietta Wentworth-Stanley for tireless typing; Sue Eldin and Barbara Robertson for efficient administration of the experimental "pilot versions"; Simon Reynolds and the Bible Society manuscript-readers for helpful comments and suggestions; Becky Totterdell and Louise Kirby for patient editing and rewriting; Mansel Connick and Angie Edge for careful proofreading; the members of the churches listed who tested the course in draft form; the Leverhulme Trust who paid his salary and expenses for the eighteen months of initial research; and, above all, Andrew Cornes who graciously allowed his lectures to be recast into group learning activities, and has given the project his wholehearted support at every stage.

Foreword

by the Rt Revd Michael Baughen

"What do you do in the church?", I asked a successful business man. "They sometimes let me carry the offertory bag", he replied. Like thousands of other Christians, his abilities are unused in the church and his God-given talents to serve Christ are untrained. Yet God expects our talents to be effectively used and not buried.

The New Testament concept of "every-member ministry" has been rediscovered, but training is seldom taken seriously (compare this with the commitment to training in sport). "Training" often consists of a few lectures rather than a properly programmed development of knowledge, talents and skills by learning, articulating, practising and "working out".

Ready to Serve is thorough training. Andrew Cornes brought high commitment to the task. To get "Core Year" (as it was originally called) right he prayed, read through and assessed other schemes across the world. He also required high commitment from those participating in the course. The results have been remarkable. Thousands of "Core Year Graduates" are now effectively serving Christ in the Church and the world.

It was soon obvious that many other churches would welcome this type of training, but Andrew Cornes could not simply be cloned! To put the content and methodology into print required special abilities. Lance Pierson has those skills. He thoroughly tested and re-tested his book in a variety of churches – from country to inner-city. One glance at this book shows his remarkable achievement.

We now have "Core Year" in a form that is adaptable and usable by any sort of church in any sort of area. I am thrilled with this production and excited at the potential of this superb course being used throughout the Church. I commend it with enthusiasm and pray that all who use it may become far more effective for Christ as they become truly "ready to serve".

+ MICHAEL CESTR:

The story behind *Ready to Serve*

In the mid-1970s All Souls' Church, Langham Place took the step of redeploying its curates as heads of different departments in the church's life. Recognizing the crucial need to train church members for practical ministry, they appointed Andrew Cornes in 1976 as their first Director of Training.

"God means every Christian without exception to have a ministry", he writes. So his training department "existed to help people discover, and develop, their abilities and gifts of service".

The basic foundation course at All Souls', intended for all Christian adults beyond the earliest, "nurture" stage of discipleship, was known as "Core Year". It consisted of thirty evening sessions, spread over three ten-week terms, a two/three-hour home study assignment each week, and two teaching and fellowship weekends during the year. It ran for ten years, and was a revision and considerable extension of an earlier Annual Training School, introduced to the church by John Stott.

The response to "Core Year" was overwhelming. From the third year of operation onwards the full complement of 130 "students" enrolled annually, and there was often a waiting list. A growing number of people from other churches also took part.

In the 1980s Lance Pierson was appointed Extension Editor, to produce a revised version of the course for use in other churches. His tasks were to shorten and adapt the material for use by congregations other than All Souls', and to convert it from lectures into a format for group learning.

He ran two pilot versions of the course, during which members of the following churches helped him to test and improve the material: All Saints', Camberwell; Basingstoke Pentecostal Church; Brunswick Parish Church, Manchester; Christ Church, Clifton, Bristol; Christ Church, Cockfosters; Christ Church, Roxeth, Harrow; Elmfield Chapel, North Harrow; Fyfield Parish Church, Ongar; Holy Trinity, Frogmore, St Albans; Knighton Evangelical Church, Leicester; Morningside Baptist Church, Edinburgh; Parish of Deane, Bolton; St Andrew's, Whitehall Park, Islington; St Barnabas', Knowle, Bristol; St Edyth's, Sea Mills, Bristol; St James', Muswell Hill; St John's, High Wycombe; St Luke's, Watford; St Mark's, Leamington Spa; St Matthew's, Fulham; St Peter's, Shipley; St Peter's, Tunbridge Wells; St Peter's, Woolton, Liverpool; and Yokine Baptist Church, Perth, Western Australia.

Their experience and comments have contributed to the developments now incorporated in this first edition of the newly named *Ready to Serve*; but, of course, they are in no way responsible for any inadequacies that remain.

This book will sometimes speak to the reader as "we". This is not Lance Pierson trying to sound royal, although as author he takes final responsibility for the book's content. But he is conscious of representing the experience of the testing churches and of generations of "Core Year Graduates", and supremely the wisdom of Andrew Cornes, the original deviser of the course.

General introduction

Welcome to *Ready to Serve*.

Aim

This is a practical training course in how to use the Bible in daily witness and service. Its motto for each member is what Paul told Timothy: "Do your best to present yourself to God as one approved, *a workman who does not need to be ashamed and who correctly handles the word of truth*" (2 Timothy 2.15, NIV, our italics). The end-product it aims at is a task-force of Christians "ready to serve" Jesus in the regular work of their churches.

The Bible is the basic textbook, and every session includes some form of Bible study. Every course member needs a Bible to work with. We recommend that they all have the same version, to prevent confusion. Quotations in this book are from the Good News Bible (abbreviated here as GNB); but activities have been tried and tested with the New International Version (NIV) as well, and should be intelligible with all the standard translations. A great knowledge of the Bible in course members is not assumed; but a hunger to learn is.

We give the Bible such prominence because we see it as the foundation document of the Christian faith. We accept what the writers sought to convey in the Scriptures: the story of God's dealings with the human race, and authoritative guidelines for the people of God on what to believe and how to live. We understand the Bible to be the one indispensable manual for training Christians in how to serve Jesus Christ. We assume an acceptance of the authority of the Bible throughout the course. We are aware that in the Church there are other understandings of the Bible as a whole, and of many of the passages we study in *Ready to Serve*. But we do not think this practical course is the place to explore countless different interpretations of the Bible. Any course leader is, of course, free to introduce other points of view wherever this would be helpful.

Who for?

The course is designed for Christian adults. It is probably too advanced for brand-new converts with no background knowledge of the Christian faith; and probably too demanding for people with obvious emotional or pastoral problems. But others, whether they have been Christians a few months or many years, should find it helpful. There is positive value in mixing together those already experienced in practical Christian ministry with those not yet actively involved in the church.

Content

The course consists of three series:

(1) **What does the Bible say about...?**
    Topics that constantly crop up as we try to help new Christians and friends who are interested in Christianity.

1. Jesus
2. Why Jesus died
3. The Bible
4. Church
5. Doubts, suffering and guidance
6. Marriage and singleness
7. The Holy Spirit

(2) Making sense of the Bible

A method to enable people to understand and explain any passage from the Bible that they come across in daily witness and service.
1. You can do it!
2. Why do people think the Bible's boring? (application)
3. Always look at the setting
4. The basic method
5. Words, words, words!
6. Inside information (historical background)
7. Picture language, poetry and parables

(3) Finding the job God wants me to do in my church

Taking the first steps of Christian ministry, in order to reach a clear idea of what God wants us to do in our church.
1. Leading a group meeting: Bible study
2. Leading a group meeting: prayer time
3. Helping other people: understanding
4. Helping other people: listening and responding
5. Outreach: telling people about Jesus
6. Speaking in public
7. What job *does* God want me to do in my church?

The theory behind these three main units or *series* is this. All the practical ministries introduced in Series 3 – leading a small fellowship group; helping other people with their problems or doubts; telling people about Jesus; and giving a lead in Sunday services – involve explaining the Bible to other people. So we first need a grounding in what the Bible says about the most frequent subjects of ordinary discussion (Series l); and in how to be sure that we are understanding the Bible (Series 2). It is not essential to take Series 1 before Series 2; you could well reverse them. Our reason for putting Series 1 first is that it can have immediate impact on relationships and conversations that are already happening. Series 2, on the other hand, puts together more gradually a method of understanding the Bible.

Course structure

Each *series* consists of seven *sessions*, each on a separate topic. Here again, the material is flexible and you are welcome to add, omit or alter individual activities or even whole sessions (unless you plan a course certificate – see p. xviii below).

For instance, there is nothing sacrosanct about the number seven. You may gain considerably by adding an eighth session of discussion and assessment at the end of the series. Alternatively, spread the series over eight sessions, by spending the first half-session introducing, and the last half-session reviewing; in between, do the first half of each new topic in the *second* half of each session, and the second half of each topic in the first half of the *next* session! This can provide useful continuity and revision from week to week.

The vital thing is to find the level and pace that best suit your course members. If, for example, a particular item captures their imagination, it could be valuable to discuss it in depth and to drop the rest of the programme. But be sensitive to the needs of your course members as a whole; don't let red herrings lead you off the track of what will benefit the majority.

Twenty-one sessions may seem many more than you could attempt, certainly in quick succession. While the course does develop a momentum when it runs straight through (spread over the three-term year, say, as in the original "Core Year" at Langham Place), this is not essential. You could do one series one year, another the next. You could select just four or five sessions each time. You could use Series 2 on its own, as part of a more general introduction to the Bible. Or you could put together "pick'n'mix" courses, using selected sessions from each series. Three simple examples might be:

Focus on the Bible

1. *Series 1, Session 3*   The Bible's teaching about itself
2. *Series 2, Session 2*   Why do people think the Bible's boring?
3. *Series 2, Session 6*   Inside information (historical background)
4. *Series 3, Session 1*   Leading a group Bible study
5. *Series 3, Session 6*   Speaking in public (focused on reading the Bible aloud)

People and their problems

1. *Series 1, Session 5*   Doubts, suffering and guidance
2. *Series 1, Session 6*   Marriage and singleness
3. *Series 2, Session 2*   Why do people think the Bible's boring?
4. *Series 3, Session 3*   Helping other people: understanding
5. *Series 3, Session 4*   Helping other people: listening and responding

---

> **Equipping for evangelism**
> 1. *Series 1, Session 1*   The Bible's teaching about Jesus
> 2. *Series 1, Session 2*   The Bible's teaching about why Jesus died
> 3. *Series 1, Session 3*   The Bible's reliability
> 4. *Series 2, Session 3*   Aways look at the setting – a key to understanding and handling the Bible accurately
> 5. *Series 3, Session 5*   Telling people about Jesus

If you try any of these approaches, you may need to adapt the material rather more than we suggest. We have not given Series 2 and 3 as gentle a start as Series 1; we have assumed that people will rise to the challenge of them when treating the course as a consecutive whole.

Level and style

The members of most churches cover a wide range of Christian experience and intellectual ability. Some of your course members will probably find this material too simple, especially early in Series 1. Encourage old-stagers to help those who are younger in the faith; developing pastoral skill is, after all, a main aim of the course. Far from being "beneath them", helping to train a younger Christian will stretch them to the full. When an activity asks you to work in pairs, don't be afraid to "arrange" them along those lines.

Meanwhile, others may find this style, which demands so much participation, strange and threatening, and may even want to drop out of the course. Do gently urge them to persevere; they really will enjoy it as they get used to it! At the start of a series, some form of commitment to see it through to the end is not a bad idea; it ensures a fair trial. You might simply explain this to everyone at the first session; or, if your church would appreciate this approach, you could organize each series as evening classes, with a booking form and a fee to cover cost of materials and overheads.

It is our conviction that adults gain most from a training course when they are able to contribute their own ideas and experience. Even if they are fairly new Christians, they probably have at least 20 years of life to reflect on; they have already learnt much from it. So *Ready to Serve* is not a set of lecture notes for a "teacher" to read to them. It is a sequence of activities in which the course members can let "Christ's message in all its richness... live in your hearts. Teach and instruct *each other* with all wisdom" (Colossians 3.16, our italics). The early sessions of Series 1 introduce this sharing of experience gently, in case it is new and demanding.

Leadership

You are not often going to be the traditional "speaker" or "discussion leader". Most of the time you should be a blend of:

(a) *Resource Person* – be familiar with the material so that you are able to answer questions, make decisions, restructure an activity, etc. Make sure that people understand each exercise and get the most out of it.

(b) *Model* – you need to demonstrate how to do some of the exercises, with an open, constructive attitude. When you tell people about your own ideas or experience, keep it simple and honest. A relaxed, co-operative atmosphere will stem from your example.

(c) *Time-keeper* – move people on from one activity to the next after the time suggested, so that it is used well and not wasted. Make sure that the fastest don't get bored, nor the slowest left behind. If you take part in an activity, appoint someone else as time-keeper.

(d) *Pastoral carer* – be on the lookout to help and reassure anyone in distress. Some will find the amount of thinking in the course hard work. Some may panic in early sessions when required to say something or write it down. Many people feel intimidated and alarmed when asked to talk about their experiences or opinions in front of others. And some people will have unhappy memories in the areas of life covered by some of the sessions in Series 1 and 3. Encourage course members to keep telling you their reactions. And do what you can to pair up quieter people with those who are more confident and outgoing.

In many ways this is *more* demanding than traditional "up front" leadership. To get the best out of a varied gathering of people requires great sensitivity and, above all, complete confidence with the material. It is essential to have worked through in advance everything that you ask the course members to do. For this reason, we estimate that it may take the leaders up to three hours to prepare each session.

It may be useful to share the leadership among two or three of you, working as a team. It would certainly be good to have at least one person of each sex as a "pastor" for course members to take any questions or problems to, even if only one of you actually leads the sessions. This style of leadership needs skill, and it takes time for the trust of the course members to build up from one session to the next. So we do *not* recommend rotating leadership around, say, members of an already established home group.

Timing

(a) Each session is timed to last one and a half hours, which we feel is the minimum useful time for training sessions on these topics.

(b) Each session is in two separate forty-five minute *blocks*. You could tackle one block per meeting, if this is as long as you want to give to it. If you decide to cover the whole session in one meeting, we recommend you to take a refreshments break between the two blocks.

(c) Each activity has a suggested timing; you need to stick to it if you are going to cover the whole session in the minimum time. But if you have got extra time available, most activities would gain from lasting a further three to five minutes.

(d) If you are doing the "Something to do at home" assignments (see page xvii below), you should allow a further fifteen minutes in each session for comments on how people got on.

Shortage of time

Many complain that they cannot cover the ground in the time. Three simple rules help:

(a) Follow the instructions about pairs, small groups, etc. If you do everything as a group of eight or ten, it will, of course, take two or three times as long as we indicate. Our philosophy is that the most effective way to build up our skills and learning is usually in a very small group.

(b) Minimize the time you spend giving instructions. Arrange your meeting room to cut down time spent on changes of seating to a matter of seconds. If an activity is at all complicated, start people on the first stage, and explain what to do next as they go along, rather than issue complete instructions at the beginning.

(c) Interrupt people before they have "finished" activities involving discussion; otherwise they will talk for as long as you let them. Don't keep the quicker members waiting. Don't hang around till the slowest reach the end; they will benefit from what they have managed to do.

Groupings

The instructions recommend a constant interchange between everyone working together (which is described as the full course) and breaking into smaller groups.

(a) If your course is very large, the full course may be too unwieldy a unit except for mini-lectures and reporting back. The rest of the time, it may be better for people to belong to permanent groups of six to twelve, with a competent leader working from this manual. Series 3 sets up small "core groups" of four members to allow everyone to practise skills in a secure, supportive atmosphere.

(b) Whenever an activity asks for small groups, it is worth trying to ensure that each group contains at least one reasonably mature, informed Christian.

(c) Some activities ask people to work in pairs. It is usually better, at least after the first session or two, not to let married couples or flatmates form a pair. They already know each other well enough, and can be a restriction on each other; experiences are better shared on a broader basis. When the instructions in the book ask people to work with their partners, it means their *Ready to Serve* colleagues, not their spouses or boy- or girlfriends!

   Obviously there will be one threesome if your group is an odd number, and often this doesn't matter. But if you feel it is important for the activity to be done in pairs, redress the balance by joining in or dropping out yourself.

(d) Some activities ask you to work on your own, but let people work in pairs if they prefer.

Introductory activity

Most blocks start with some form of relaxed activity, which will help to make the course members feel more comfortable with one another, as well as introduce the main topic. This is suggested because we are trying to create the depth of trust and support in which learning can take place easily. Even one week's break since you last met creates a layer of shyness and reserve between people; you need to thaw it out gently to get back to where you were. These activities are not essential and some people may think them trivial or distracting. The material is certainly wrong for people on your course if it leaves several feeling stupid or embarrassed; but our usual experience is that Bible study flows more smoothly as a result of these activities.

Members' pages

Ready to Serve is divided into leader's and members' pages. All members' pages and handout pages are photocopiable and can be distributed to those taking part in the *Ready to Serve* course. Copyright restrictions as stated at the beginning of this book apply to all other pages. Each course member needs their own copy of the members' pages. They form the members' own record of all they are learning. Each block contains at least one activity on these pages. Usually this is done alone or in small groups. But sometimes people will want to take notes on activities not referred to on the members' pages. For this reason it is always good if you can show a visual list of your main headings, or of any ideas that the course members report back from a discussion; so you will need a board, flipchart, or overhead projector (OHP).

Drama and role play

Drama and role play are used fairly frequently through the course. Some people are naturally shy, so we introduce these techniques gently in the early sessions of Series 1. None of the activities requires great dramatic skill or experience.

The dramatic sketches in *Ready to Serve* come with a script for you to photocopy and give to suitable people to read. They make a situation visible and objective, so that you can talk about it more easily. "Role play" asks people to imagine a situation and to act out what they would do or say in it. When reasuringly explained and demonstrated, it is the most basic way to get practice and feedback, and is absolutely essential in practical training. It brings the subject down to earth and gives people the chance to explore it in a safe and sympathetic environment. Discussing afterwards what went well or what went wrong allows real learning and progress to take place. It can also be great fun!

You may decide to introduce it more gently than is suggested, but unless you reach the point where everybody has a trial run at putting what they believe into their own words, you have not trained them to serve Jesus – you have merely stocked their minds with more information.

Finishing the session

In sessions 1, 2 and 3 of Series 1, we suggest that each block should end with praise and song, or reflection and prayer, or questions and discussion. Elsewhere we have not usually timetabled these, but one or more of them is always a good way to round off a session of learning and training.

"Something to do at home"

We feel there is *great loss* (perhaps 50 per cent of the course's value) if people are not putting what they have learnt into practice, and continuing the train of thought, between sessions. So there is a range of assignments with each series.

You will find them at the end of each series. There is a simple "Basic Level", and in Series 1 and 2 there is an "Advanced Level" for people who are more experienced; you might consider using it if you plan a course certificate (see below). Or you may prefer to ask people to complete or prepare items in the Members' pages, if there is not time to cover them in the sessions.

Course certificate

We see considerable value in working through the course for some form of certificate or qualification. It provides an incentive for the personal discipline and commitment required by the course. It also recognizes that people have achieved a standard, which we hope will improve the quality of lay minsitry (not only in your church but in any that course members may later move to).

So we encourage you to produce a means of recognition to award to all who complete the course. This might grow into a standard requirement for office-holders and team members in your church, and could even be run jointly with some neighbouring churches, so that you recognize and share each other's trained workers.

If you do implement this sort of scheme you would be wise to demand some minimum requirements before awarding a certificate. One example might be:

(a) The course leader(s) in signing the certificate is certifying that this trainee has:
    (i) completed all three series;
    (ii) attended at least six sessions in each series;
    (iii) produced written home assignments at "Advanced" level for at least five sessions in each series.

(b) An appropriate team leader must certify that the trainee has:
    (i) been incorporated into an area of service recognized by the church, for which her/his abilities equip her/him;
    (ii) already received (or will within the next year) further training designed for this area of service;
    (iii) satisfactorily completed six probationary months in this area of service before, during or after the training course.

What does the Bible say about . . .?

Introduction

Aim

Do not let the series title "What does the Bible say about...?" mislead you. This is not a series on Bible teaching as an end in itself. It does not work through the books of the Bible or the creeds. Nor does it try to present everything that the Bible says on each topic. It is a purpose-built part of the whole course, *Ready to Serve*. It tries to equip course members with the Bible knowledge they need to answer the sort of questions most commonly raised by the people they will most naturally know and meet – some already Christians, but others not.

As we talk to new Christians and friends who are interested in Christianity, some subjects crop up again and again. This series of seven sessions looks at some of what the Bible says about these subjects. Each session aims to help us understand its subject *in order to pass on* this understanding to our friends. This course is training us to help other people; it cannot always go far enough or deep enough into each subject to answer *all* our questions. So each session starts with Bible study, and then has at least one exercise which involves a practical attempt to explain Bible truth to someone else.

We give so much time and importance to the Bible, because we believe it is the one indispensable textbook of the Christian faith. In our experience, course members will have much less success in helping other people understand Christianity if they simply air their own, independent opinions. They need to be able to grasp and then express the truths about God, Jesus and the world which run all through the Bible. We are, of course, aware that some Christians today interpret the Bible, and the subjects in this series, differently; as leader, you may find it helpful to refer to them.

The method by which we reach our understanding of the Bible here is spelt out in detail in Series 2. You may prefer to start the course at that point. Our reason for starting here is that we want course members to feel equipped and *ready* to *serve* other people (and the questions they are asking) from the very first session.

Content

The topics for the seven sessions are:
1. Jesus
2. Why Jesus died
3. The Bible
4. Church
5. Doubts, suffering and guidance
6. Marriage and singleness
7. The Holy Spirit

These are not necessarily the most important topics in the Christian faith. But in our experience, they are the most common talking points among the new Christians and outsiders we are seeking to serve.

There is nothing God-given about this order of the topics. You may, with good reason, prefer to take them in a different order. But the sessions have been designed on the assumption that they will run in the printed order (1 introduces the series, 7 sums it up, etc.) If you change the order, you may also need to make minor adjustments to the sessions, to help them flow from one to the next.

Bible study methods

These vary from session to session; different people prefer different approaches, so there should be something to suit everyone. The aim is always to help people discover Bible truth for themselves, *in order to use it and pass it on*.

Something to do at home

You need to decide:

(a) whether to set people some assignments to keep their minds on the course between sessions;

(b) whether to make them voluntary or "three-line whip";

(c) whether to choose Basic Level (Members' pages 80–88) or Advanced (pages 88–91), or to give people the choice;

(d) whether to do something else, such as completing or preparing an activity in the session.

The Advanced Level projects list three or four Bible passages on each topic. They enable people to read a fuller range of what the Bible says than is possible in the sessions themselves. They would therefore make a worthwhile home study task in their own right, if people do not do the suggested written exercise.

If you do set written work, we recommend that *somebody* reads it through and comments on it each time. If this is too big a load for you as leader every time, it is often helpful for pairs or threes to look at each other's. This is suggested for some of the sessions.

■ **Session 1** ■

Jesus

AIM

We begin the course by looking at some of the Bible's teaching about Jesus, not simply because he is Lord. Our aim throughout this first series is to learn how to pass on the particular Bible truths that will help new Christians to grow, and enquirers to find faith. Jesus himself is, of course, at the heart of our good news for both groups of people. Block 1 concentrates on who Jesus claimed to be; Block 2 on the fact that Jesus Christ lives today.

BLOCK 1: GOD AND MAN

1. Who is Jesus?

Introductory thought-starter

10 mins

Start by getting the group to think about the uniqueness of Jesus and how they account for it.

Prepare a good reader to read aloud the piece called "One Solitary Life" on page 8. Then introduce general discussion for 3 to 4 minutes, using one of these methods:

(a) Simply ask: "Why has Jesus had such a huge influence on the history of the world?"

(b) If you think the course members will need more encouragement to start talking, divide them into small groups of two or three to discuss the question.

(c) If you think they would prefer to be more passive at this stage, prepare an extrovert character to discuss the question with you in front of the others; they would benefit from seeing "One Solitary Life" in advance. One of you should play devil's advocate, using any argument you can think of to avoid the Christian conclusion that Jesus is God become man. Finish by asking everyone which of the two they found more convincing!

(d) If you have *several* extrovert characters, get them to conduct a tape-recorded survey in the street or maret place, asking passers by: "Who do you think Jesus was?" A selection of their replies would make lively listening. Hold a brief discussion after playing the tape.

2. What he said, and who he was

Programmed Bible study

30 mins

Distribute a copy of this section from the members' pages to everyone. Explain that you are about to try what experts say is one of the most effective ways of learning. It is called "programmed learning" because the information is arranged in an order or programme, carefully chosen to make sense of the material and to help the memory. In addition, writing answers down means that they have to be thought out clearly beforehand.

Look at the goals and instructions under "input" together. Check that everyone has understood. Then leave them to work at their own speed, in pairs or alone, whichever they prefer.

As leader, you should be a "resource person" and go round the room, checking that everyone is making progress happily, giving help where needed. Interrupt every 10 minutes to ask out loud whether people are getting on all right. Note – in question (1a) we understand "The Father and I are one" (John 10.30) to include "I am God just as much as my Father is" (third statement) as well as the second statement; but not "we are one and the same person" (first statement).

Stop after half an hour. It does *not* matter if people have not finished; the value is in the ground they *have* covered.

The quiz at the end is only really intended for the quick workers; but it would be good to go through

LEADER'S NOTES

it orally all together to round off this activity. In particular, encourage course members to start thinking who they might be able to help (new Christians or interested enquirers) by passing on the Bible information they have gleaned.

Be prepared for both these common reactions:

(a) this activity skates over the surface, and is too simplistic;
(b) it is hard work, and too "schooly".

If you get both on the same course, it shows how mixed our churches are, educationally and spiritually; and underlines the need for sensitive partnering of "mature" with "young" Christians in future sessions. The programmed learning method is not often used in the course. People who have received

further education may well find it restrictive and mechanical. They do not always appreciate that others need something like this to follow a line of argument and form a reasoned opinion. We use this method in the first session to give people some input before asking for their own ideas and experiences in Block 2.

3. Praise

Song   5 mins

Choose a song of praise and perhaps follow it with a few moments for people to say their own short prayers of praise to Jesus as Lord and God. Or let them choose another song, and say what they like about it.

BLOCK 2: DEAD BUT NOW LIVING

1. Jesus Christ is alive

Reading   5 mins

All Jesus' miracles point to the fact that he was God as well as man. But the supreme miracle is his resurrection from the dead; so the first part of Block 2 concentrates on that. This is the crowning proof that Jesus is more than a mere human being. "... He was shown with great power to be the son of God by being raised from death" (Romans 1.4).

As an introduction to the subject, ask two good readers to read (having prepared in advance) the item "Jesus Christ is alive" on page 9.

Ask people what exactly they understand by the words, "Jesus is alive". What, for instance, do they make of the view that he is only "alive" in the sense that his example and wishes live on in the lives of his followers and worshippers?

2. How do we know that Jesus Christ lives?

Bible research   15 mins

Move people on to the activity on pages 14–16 in this section's members' pages. Divide the full course into at least three groups and give each group one of the "sleuth" assignments.

The question in each case is: Does the common "explanation" of Jesus' resurrection fit the facts? In the verdict box they should write either "agree" or "disagree".

Allow three minutes at the end of this activity for each group to report their verdict, and the reasons for it, to the others.

3. Jesus Christ lives today

Sharing   10 mins

If death really couldn't hold Jesus down, then presumably he must be living and active today. For Christians this should not be an irrelevant fact; it should make all the difference in the world to how we live.

So ask people, in pairs, to share together what kind of difference Jesus is making to their lives today. If any find this question difficult to understand, rephrase it as, "In what ways would your life be different if you were not a Christian?".

After four minutes, ask them to change round and let the other partner have a turn.

When they have finished, perhaps have a few moments of quiet for everyone to take in afresh that our Lord Jesus Christ is alive and present. Or perhaps ask people to suggest a few quick ideas to help us all remember more often that he is alive and with us.

4. Christ in my life

Role play   10 mins

Explain that *some* people who are not Christians like to avoid the main issues of Christianity by raising red herrings: topics they are not really interested in, but which can distract us from talking personally about our faith. (But do stress that not *all* "non-Christians" are like this; many have honest, valid reasons for not sharing our beliefs.)

As the living Christ is the heart of Christianity, it is often better in such circumstances to talk about him, rather than about "faith" or "Christianity", which can be very vague. It is far easier to relate to a personality than an idea. Talking about how Christ helps you may be the best way of giving the other person confidence to ask about God's answer to their own needs.

To demonstrate the point, bring together four reasonably mature Christians who are happy to "act" in front of others – by all means include yourself. Ask everyone else to watch and enjoy themselves, while the four act out a conversation between two Christians and two of their friends who are not Christians. Ideally, this should be spontaneous, but prepare in advance if it would give more confidence.

Give the two "non-Christians" one of these conversation-starters:

(a) "We went past your church last Sunday morning, but couldn't see anyone. Does anybody actually go there?"

(b) "The people who go to church round our area are such hypocrites. You should see what the Buggins get up to!"

(c) "The trouble with this country is that it's going to the dogs. It's a pity there aren't more people like you around, with high moral standards."

(d) "Some of the Church's own bishops say they don't believe the Bible, don't they?"

From that opening the "Christians" should try to lead the conversation round to Jesus, while the "non-Christians" talk and react in keeping with their character.

After five minutes, stop the conversation, wherever it has got to, and give the four participants a few moments to unwind and get back into their real selves. Ask them how the experience felt and how they would change what they said if they had the chance to hold the conversation again. Ask the other course members for any comments or suggestions: have they heard their friends say similar things? What have they themselves said in similar conversations?

5. Reflection

5 mins

Ask everyone to take two to three minutes to think back over the session as a whole, and then respond to God – silently – about the main thing that has struck them. Then say a closing prayer yourself.

One Solitary Life

He was born of Jewish parents in an obscure village – the child of a peasant woman. He grew up in another obscure village where he worked in a carpenter's shop till he was 30, and then for three years became an itinerant preacher.

He never wrote a book; he never held office; he never owned a house; he never had a family. He never went to college. He never travelled more than 200 miles from the place where he was born. He never did one of the things that usually accompany greatness. He had no credentials but himself.

While he was still a young man, the tide of popular opinion turned against him. His friends ran away; one betrayed him, one denied him. He was turned over to his enemies and went through a mockery of a trial.

He was nailed to a cross between two thieves. His executioners gambled for the only piece of property he owned on earth – and that was his robe.

When he was dead he was taken down and laid in a borrowed grave, through the pity of a friend.

Nineteen centuries have come and gone, and today he is the centre-piece of the human race and the inspiration of most progress in civilization.

I am well within the mark when I say that:
    all the armies that ever marched
    all the navies that sailed the seas
    all the Parliaments that ever sat, and
    all the kings that ever reigned, put together,
have not affected the destiny of the human race as powerfully as has *that one solitary life*.

Anon

8

Jesus Christ is Alive

∙∙∙

READER l: Jesus Christ is alive.

READER 2: The Queen is alive, Prince Charles is alive,
Prince William is alive.

1:      Jesus is alive.

2:      [Name of Prime Minister] is alive, [Name of leader of Opposition]
is alive, [Name of third party leader] is alive.

1:      Jesus is alive.

2:      (*In the same rhythm, use the names of three of your own
church/course*)
X is alive, Y is alive, Z is alive.

1:      Jesus is alive.

2:      Barabbas is dead.

1:      Jesus is alive.

2:      Caesar is dead, Mohammed is dead, Karl Marx is dead,
Charles Darwin is dead.

1:      Jesus is alive.

2:      Confucius, he say, he dead.

1:      Jesus is alive.

2:      You are living –

1:      Jesus is living –

1&2 (*together*): Jesus is alive!

Adapted from *Jesus is alive*, written by the Kairos group, © John Wilson
1972. Published by Falcon, but now out of print. Alter the details to
make them up-to-date and relevant to your course.

Jesus

BLOCK 1: GOD AND MAN

■ What he said, and who he was

GOALS
By the end of this study you will be able to put into words:
- *three ways that Jesus claimed to be God;*
- *three witnesses to his perfect character.*

INPUT
Work through the following sections at your own speed. Each contains some information and some questions to answer. Each section adds to what you have learnt previously.

1. Jesus claimed to be God come to earth

(a) Sometimes he made *direct claims* to be God.
For example, look up John 10.27–30. Jesus is speaking to some Jewish leaders who have asked him if he is the promised Messiah. Tick any of these which you think Jesus meant by the words in verse 30:

☐ God the Father and I are one and the same person.

☐ God the Father and I like the same things.

☐ I am God just as much as my Father in heaven is.

Read on to verses 31–33. What do the Jews say that makes it clear they knew Jesus had directly claimed to be God?

....

....

....

....

(b) Sometimes he made *indirect claims* to be God; i.e. he did not contradict those who regarded him as God or realized that only God could do the things that Jesus was doing.
For example, look up John 20.26–29, the events a week after Jesus' resurrection. Thomas had not witnessed Jesus' first appearance alive after

death, and doubted whether it was true. Tick which of these Thomas said when Jesus spoke to him:

☐ "It's a ghost!"

☐ "Good Lord!"

☐ "My Lord and my God!"

In verse 29 Jesus accepts Thomas calling him God. The God of the whole universe has:

☐ the right to be worshipped by human beings;

☐ the right to forgive their sins;

☐ the right to judge their lives.

Tick which of those three rights you think Thomas' words in verse 28 show him recognizing in Jesus.

(c) For another example of an indirect claim to be God, look up Matthew 7.21–23. These are words of warning at the end of Jesus' Sermon on the Mount.
What is the "day" Jesus refers to?

....

This shows Jesus claiming God's right (tick one):

☐ to be worshipped;

☐ to forgive sins;

☐ to judge men and women.

(d) **RECAP**

Write down three claims made by Jesus to be God (either in his words or your own):

(i)   Direct: ....

....

(ii) Indirect: ....

....

(iii) Indirect:...

....

2. Jesus backed up his claims by his perfect character

Anyone claiming to be God must be sinless, as God is.

(a) Look up John chapter 8. It is the record of a long argument between Jesus and the Jews.

From verse 29, write down the words of Jesus that clearly show him claiming to be without sin:

....

....

(b) Look at Jesus' challenge in the first half of verse 46. Read through verses 31–59 and list any sins that they successfully pin on Jesus:

....

....

(c) The New Testament claims that Jesus never sinned. His enemies were unable to find any instance of him doing wrong.

Tick which of the following probably knows most about your faults:

☐ your husband/wife/mother

☐ your bank manager

☐ the Prime Minister

☐ your best friend

Generally, those who live closest to us know us best. And they'd be most unlikely to say that we'd never done anything wrong. But write down what Jesus' closest friends said about him:

Peter – in 1 Peter 2.21–23

....

....

....

John – in 1 John 3.5

....

....

(d) RECAP

So who are the three witnesses (or groups of witnesses) to Jesus' perfect character?

(i) .... (section (a))

(ii) His enemies   (section (b))

(iii) .... (section (c))

3. Quiz

Can you remember?

(a) Two indirect ways in which Jesus claimed to be God:

(i) ....

....

(ii) ....

....

(b) Two groups of people, other than Jesus himself, who found that his character was perfect:

(i) ....

(ii) ....

Can you think of one or two people you know, who would find it a real help to know these claims which the Bible makes about Jesus?

(i) ....

(ii) ....

Jesus

BLOCK 2: DEAD BUT NOW LIVING

■ How do we know that Jesus Christ lives?

Be your own Sherlock Holmes!

Sleuth assignment

A "Jesus didn't actually die on the cross."
As a group, decide whether this theory that Jesus didn't die on the cross fits the facts.
Study the evidence and implications in:

> John 19.31–35
> Mark 15.42–47
> Luke 24.36–43
> Luke 24.50–52

(Share out the passages around your group.)
Clues in favour of the theory:

1. ....

2. ....

3. ....

4. ....

Clues against the theory:

1. ....

2. ....

3. ....

4. ....

Your verdict: ....

Sleuth assignment ✓

B "Jesus' so-called appearances were hallucinations."
As a group, detect whether this theory that Jesus did not really appear to his followers alive fits the facts.
Study the evidence and implications in:

John	20.11–29
Luke	24.36–43
Acts	1.1–3
1 Corinthians	15.3–8

(Share out the passages around your group.)
Clues in favour of the theory:

1. ....

2. ....

3. ....

4. ....

Clues against the theory:

1. ....

2. ....

3. ....

4. ....

Your verdict: ....

Sleuth assignment ✓

C "The disciples made up the story of the resurrection."
As a group, detect whether this theory that Jesus did not really come back to life fits the facts.
Study the evidence and implications in:

Mark	8.27–33
Mark	14.43–50
Luke	24.13–35, 44–49
Acts	2.5–15, 29–33, 43–47

(Share out the passages around your group.)

Clues in favour of the theory:

1. ....

2. ....

3. ....

4. ....

Clues against the theory:

1. ....

2. ....

3. ....

4. ....

Your verdict: ....

■ Session 2 ■

Why Jesus died

AIM

Following the first session's study of who Jesus is, this session takes a close-up look at the supreme task he came to do. It may seem strange at first sight to look at Jesus' death after spending time on his resurrection in Session 1. But we are taking these events not in chronological order, but as parts of the Christian Good News that we are learning to share with new Christians, and with friends who are showing interest in Christianity. In practice we shall often find that we discuss who Jesus was and is before discussing what he came to do. Jesus' death on the cross is, of course, at the very heart of this, and merits a session in itself.

BLOCK 1: CROSS-PURPOSES

1. Why did Jesus come?

Discussion and input

 10 mins

Ask people in groups of two or three to look at page 19 from the members' pages, and write down how they would complete the sentence: "The main reason why Jesus came to earth was ... ."

Give them up to five minutes for this; then hear some or all of the answers without commenting on them beyond thanking people for their contributions.

Then sum up that one of the main reasons Jesus himself gave was: in order to die. Ask someone to read Mark 10.45 and John 12.27–28 to demonstrate the point. Finish by stressing that it was death for a good purpose!

2. Close-up on the cross

Bible study

 30 mins

Pages 19–24 contain nine Bible passages about Jesus' death on the cross. The aim is to survey some of the breadth of New Testament teaching about the cross, before focusing in Block 2 on how to present it. According to what will work best with the number of people on your course, decide whether to

cover all the passages or only some of them. They start with some points about the example Jesus set us, before coming to his death on the cross for us. Some are harder to understand than others, especially *d*, *h* and *i*; make yourself available to explain these or any other passages which raise questions. Assign one passage each to an individual, or a pair, or a small group, and let them work on the questions for fifteen minutes. If they finish early, they can move on to another passage.

Then ask them to complete the final sentence on page 24 "For everyone", and be ready to read it out. As you hear what they have written, try briefly to draw out of them how the passage in question brought that particular insight to light.

3. Praise

 5 mins

Close this block with open prayer and perhaps a song about Jesus' death, such as "When I survey the wondrous cross", or "From heaven you came, helpless babe" ("The Servant King"). Encourage people to express some of their wonder and thanksgiving at what Jesus did for us. Tell people that you will be thinking more in Block 2 about what the cross means.

BLOCK 2: CROSS-TALK

Block 2 starts by summing up the New Testament teaching about Jesus' death from Block 1, but then spends most of its time on how to talk about the cross to others.

1. The message of the cross

Bible study and short talk   10 mins

Start Block 2 by all looking together at some more of Paul's teaching about Jesus' death. Try to pull together and build on what people have contributed in Block 1. Ask them to look up 1 Corinthians 1.17–18 and 2.1–5, and arrange for a good reader to read it aloud. Then ask:

"Paul says he decided to preach about nothing except Jesus and his crucifixion (2.2). How can this 'message of the cross' (1.18), be the complete 'Good News' (1.17)? Why is it not necessary to know or tell anything else in explaining to someone how to become a Christian?"

Either draw out in Bible study, or point out in a short talk, some of these truths:

(a) The cross shows up the depth of our sin, in that Jesus needed to die for us (2 Corinthians 5.21).

(b) The cross shows up God's love, in that Jesus willingly died for us (Romans 5.8).

(c) The fact that Jesus died for us on the cross means that we can be fully forgiven for our sin (Romans 4.25).

(d) Because Jesus' offering on the cross was perfect, he has removed the barrier between us and God, and we are able to start a new life in his family (1 Peter 2.24–25).

(e) The impact of the cross on us is to encourage us to give ourselves to Jesus in return (2 Corinthians 5.14–15).

Select two or three key points and do not spend too long on this. Your aim is to sum up the input from Block 1, to help people work on activity (2) below. Sum up that Jesus' death for us on the cross is at the heart of the Good News. If we can learn to explain it to people, we shall be well equipped to help them become Christians. Even then, of course, we need to rely prayerfully on the Holy Spirit to bring the words home to them (1 Corinthians 2.4–5).

2. Putting it across

Task groups   30 mins

Divide people into four groups, and assign each of them one of the "target groups" on page 25 of the members' pages. Ask them to work out a suitable way of explaining the good news of Jesus' death to a group of either children, teenagers, working adults or parents of young children. They should focus on the members of the group who have not yet come to Christian faith. In particular, they should try to think of a good "illustration" (i.e., a story, example or parallel experience) that will make sense to that segment of the population, and help them to understand the Good News more clearly. For example, the New Testament often explains Jesus' death in terms of animal sacrifice; it is an idea that needs explaining or illustrating in other terms in the twentieth century, because it is not part of our experience whereas for Jews of New Testament times it would have been something people could relate to and understand. Members should work out in as much detail as they can how they would present their illustration.

After 15 to 20 minutes, hear the ideas from each group.

3. Prayer

5 mins

Close this block all together, or in the task groups, praying for opportunities to spread this Good News, or for particular people who need to hear it.

SESSION 2
Why Jesus died

BLOCK 1: CROSS-PURPOSES

■ Why did Jesus come?

The main reason why Jesus came to earth was

....

....

■ Close-up on the cross

Jesus on the cross shows:

(a) His humble obedience

Look up Philippians 2.5–8
How do you think that Jesus knew that it was God's will or command for him
to die on the cross?

....

....

Can you remember any occasions when he said he *had* to die that way?

....

....

Draw a diagram of the self-humbling process he went through, as described in
these verses:

If you are going to have a Christlike attitude, what might be the next step you could take to become more humble?

....

....

(b) His ungrumbling acceptance

Look up Matthew 26.36–46
Trace how Jesus becomes more and more able to accept God's will as he prays. What are the favourite topics of grumbling in your family or church?

....

....

....

....

....

Put a cross against the situations that you have probably got to learn prayerfully to accept.

(c) His utter dedication

Look up Matthew 16.21–25
Why does Jesus call Peter "Satan"?

....

What do you think Jesus felt at that moment?

....

....

Think of an example of what it would really mean in the next week for you to:

"Forget" yourself ....

Take up and carry your cross ....

Follow Jesus ....

How dedicated are you as a disciple?

(d) His unlimited self-giving

Look up Galatians 3.10–14
Try to think of a diagram or picture, words or sounds, colours or music, or other comparisons which will, in some way, express the incredible depths Jesus went to for us. If possible or helpful, draw, compose or write them here:

How might you be able to use them in explaining to someone else why Jesus' death on the cross is good news?

(e) Jesus' lack of resentment

Look up 1 Peter 2.20–23
List and share any things you deeply resent or have resented:

....

....

....

....

....

Tick any which you can honestly say involved suffering you did not deserve. Star any where you kept your resentment to yourself and God. Compare yourself with Jesus.

(f) His unselfishness

Look up Matthew 27.35–43
Work out what thoughts you think may have run through Jesus' mind as he heard these jeers from the religious leaders:

....

....

....

....

List any common social problems you are aware of that could be solved if people learnt to be as unselfish as Jesus on the cross:

....

....

....

....

(g) His deep friendship

Look up John 15.9–17
What qualities do you look for in a friend?

....

....

....

What's your reaction to the fact that Jesus counts you as one of his friends?

....

....

....

He proved his friendship by dying in your place.

(h) God's love

Look up Romans 5.6–10
In case we think that in some way we are indispensable to God, pick out the words or phrases in these verses that describe what we were like when God first set his love on us:

....

....

....

....

How would you explain this passage to reassure a younger Christian who has said, "I understand God loving some of the really caring people in our church, but I don't see why he should love me"?

....

....

....

....

....

(i) God's justice

Look carefully at Romans 3.22–26, and then home in on the last two verses. You may need to think hard to work out what they mean! Try to put into your own words how these verses answer the question:
"How can God be a God of love and yet condemn people to hell?"

....

....

....

....

Think about it! Paul's problem was probably much more:
"How can God be a God of justice and yet forgive people?"

■ For everyone

One thing that has struck me about Jesus' death through looking at this passage is:

....

....

....

SERIES 1 / WHAT DOES THE BIBLE SAY ABOUT . . . ?

BLOCK 2 / PAGE 1

Why Jesus died

BLOCK 2: CROSS-TALK

■ Putting it across

"Tell the Good News" . . . "the message about Christ's death on the cross" . . . "Jesus Christ and especially his death on the cross".

How would you explain the good news that Jesus died for them to one of the target groups below? Try to include a clear, modern illustration of the points you are making. (Write your ideas below in note form.)

Target groups:
- children
- teenagers
- working adults (perhaps office contacts or people at an outreach supper)
- parents of very young children (perhaps from a "Parent and Toddler" group)

For **Ready to Serve** course use only © Bible Society 1995

■ **Session 3** ■

The Bible

AIM

"What does the Bible say about the Bible?" may sound a rather pointless question. But it is important for the two groups of people we are learning to help. New Christians need to know why they should listen to the Bible's teaching and obey it; and those who are not yet Christians need some reassurance that it is not a collection of legends and fairy-tales.

As explained in the Introduction, we accept the Bible writers' own view of Scripture as containing God's authoritative instructions for his people. There are, however, many views of the Bible in the Church today; if you want to introduce them you can do so in the discussion and question sessions at the end of each block.

BLOCK 1: INSTRUCTIONS FOR CHRISTIANS

1. The maker's instructions

Demonstration   5 mins

The point of this opening activity is briefly to establish the need for instruction manuals.

Introduce a complicated piece of machinery or mechanical task (for example, a food mixer, setting a VCR to record, or adjusting the time on a digital watch). Ask two people to try to make it work in front of everyone else. Make the first one use guesswork; give the second one the book of instructions.

At the end, make sure that everyone has got hold of the point of the introductory activity: *we need instructions in order to make sense of life.* Then make the point that God has given us in the Bible his maker's instructions on how to live. Perhaps quote Paul's claim in 2 Timothy 3.16 that "All Scripture is inspired by God and is useful for... giving instruction for right living", as GNB translates it. If your course did the basic level home assignment, they will have studied this verse. If they did the advanced level assignment, check that something along these lines was their main finding.

2. The Old Testament rules OK!

Bible study   20 mins

Give everyone a copy of pages 29–30 from the members' pages. The three sections are arranged so that people study on their own, with a partner,

and in a group. In section (1), allow anybody who would find it hard to read and study on their own to work with a more experienced partner.

Each section contains a basic and an extra portion; the latter is in square brackets. The aim is for everyone to complete the basic portion in 5 minutes; fast workers can go on to the extra part. After 4 minutes on each section, interrupt gently to check that everyone is getting on all right.

In section (1) watch that people don't get sidetracked into an interesting discussion of Genesis 2.24 itself! They will have the chance for that in Session 6 of this series. In this session we are simply looking at what Jesus teaches about the Bible; often he does this incidentally, as here, while giving teaching about something else.

Our suggested answers to the extra portions in section (3) are:

(1) Isaiah 53.7–8; Psalm 41.9; Zechariah 13.7.
(2) Verses 6 and 7, where the devil quotes Bible verses which seem to fit (Psalm 91.11–12), but Jesus counters with a more general biblical principle (Deuteronomy 6.16).

3. The New Testament rules OK!

Flow chart   15 mins

Explain that the evidence for the New Testament carrying God's authority as much as the Old does is cumulative; each point of evidence flows from the one before. Put all together, they make a convincing case.

Introduce the flow chart on pages 32–33. It operates at two levels:

- the main facts (1 (a), (b), (c), (d), 2, 3.)
- reasons for these facts or examples to help explain them (information in the dotted boxes leading from them).

Ask them to read it through carefully on their own, and fill in the blanks. Explain that in the 15 minutes available they may only have time to look at the main points under each heading (in the boxes with continuous sides). Suggest that, if they have time, they go back and look at the reasons and examples in the dotted boxes.

4. General discussion

5 mins

Pause at this point to air any comments and questions from your course members. Try to include some thought on how to help new Christians to make best use of the Bible.

BLOCK 2: INFORMATION FOR ENQUIRERS

1. How not to handle the Bible with the unconvinced!

Drama sketch

5 mins

Prepare two good readers to read the script on page 31.

Introduce the two characters to everyone else, using the description at the top of the script. Ask the audience to watch carefully for what is wrong in the way B uses the Bible with someone who is not a Christian.

After the sketch, ask for their suggestions. They will spot inappropriate ways of treating other people, but focus only on the bad use of the Bible. E.g.

(a) using it like a battering ram to force someone into faith;

(b) using it like a computer program to work through step-by-step;

(c) quoting its exact words and chapter numbers, which will mean nothing to someone who is not a Christian;

(d) referring to its teaching in Christian "jargon" or technical language which they won't understand;

(e) expecting someone who is not a Christian to read the Bible on their own without help;

(f) using an old, difficult translation.

2. The Bible's unique power

Input

5 mins

Put the following into your own words:

It is obviously wrong to thump people insensitively with the Bible, as character B in the sketch did. But it is also a mistake to drop the Bible altogether from our conversation with those who are not Christians.

Look at Luke 16.27–31, the end of the story of the rich man and Lazarus. Jesus says that the Scriptures have greater power to convince than even the most striking miracle.

It is only reasonable to show or tell an interested enquirer what the foundation document of Christianity says, but they will often need you to reassure them that the Bible is genuinely reliable. Many people have picked up the idea that "You can't trust the Bible".

3. Objections to the Bible

Role play

25 mins

(a) But it was all written down long after!

5 mins

Ask four reasonably confident people to perform a role play; two arguing that the Bible is unreliable, and two defending it. Ideally this should be spontaneous, but allow them to prepare in advance if you think it would help. In either event, ask them to use the arguments laid out on pages 34 and 35 of the members' pages (*a* and *a1*).

Ask everyone to follow those pages and to watch how the defenders use the arguments in box (a1). After 3 or 4 minutes, stop the role play and ask the audience who used the points in (a1) and when. Make no further comments on the role play at this stage.

(b) But what about all the contradictions?

10 mins

Ask the four to continue their public argument, now on the subject of the contradictions in the Bible. Again, two should be "objectors", using one or more of the ideas from section (b) on page 34;

and the other two should be "defenders" making use of section (b1) on page 35.

Let them hold the conversation for 5 minutes. Then, for a further 5 minutes, discuss with them how they felt, and ask for anyone else's ideas on what else the "defenders" could have said.

As leader, it may be helpful for you to comment on how the role play went *as role play*. This will help people get maximum benefit from this type of activity. Ask questions like, "Was the conversation realistic?" "Were the actors listening to each other and answering each other?" "Did the objectors let the defenders get off lightly, or were they unreasonably stubborn?"

(c,d,e) Miracles, bias and proof

10 mins

Ask everyone to divide into groups of three or four (two defenders and two objectors, or only one objector if she or he is "clued up" in the arguments against the Bible's reliability). Give each group *one* of the remaining objections to cover (c, d or e). Ask them to look only at the relevant page (34 *or* 35), so that they don't see what the others are going to say!

They should only use these ideas, if they can't think of better ones of their own. If anyone working alone now decides they want a partner to work with, let them have one. Reassure them that it will only be for 3 minutes.

After that time, take another 5 minutes for a report back on how they got on, and on any other ideas for what defenders could say. Encourage course members to report on genuine questions or opinions of their friends who are not Christians. People could make a note of anything useful.

4. Question panel

10 mins

The authority and reliability of the Bible are such fundamental, yet controversial, issues that it is worth allowing time for questions. Try to focus on how we can enter into helpful discussion with people whose starting-point is that the Bible is not reliable. Unless you are confident about the subject, it might be helpful to invite a local theological "expert" (e.g. one of your church's regular preachers) to help you comment on the questions.

The Bible

BLOCK 1: INSTRUCTIONS FOR CHRISTIANS

■ The Old Testament rules OK!

Although the Old Testament is often unpopular, Jesus clearly treated it as God's instructions for the human race, and for him personally.

1. Jesus taught that what the Old Testament says, God says

(Study this on your own)
Look up Matthew 19.3–5.
According to Jesus, who first said the words of verse 5?

....

But now look up Genesis 2.23–24, where these words come in the Old Testament. Who seems to be saying them here?

....

So it seems reasonable to conclude that, for Jesus, the Old Testament writers expressed God's thoughts even when writing their own words.

[If you have time: look up Mark 7.9–13 and 12.36, where Jesus makes the same claim about other Old Testament writers.

In Mark 7.9–13 the Old Testament writer is ....

In Mark 12.36 the Old Testament writer is ....]

2. Jesus believed that the Old Testament's moral instructions were binding

(Study this with one other person.)
Look up Matthew 5.17–19.
According to verse 18, what percentage of the Old Testament Law would you say Jesus allows people to drop?

....

This is one reason why Christians believe that God "inspired" (i.e. caused people to write) every word of the Bible exactly as he wants it.
[If you have time: look on to verses 21–22.

People sometimes say that in the Sermon on the Mount, Jesus contradicted the Old Testament Law. But what is he really doing here? How is this an example of what he said he would do in verse 17?]

3. Jesus moulded his life by obeying the Old Testament

(Study this together in groups of five or six)

(a) What he came to do

Look up Matthew 26.47–56.

Which *two* verses show that Jesus took his orders for his work from the Old Testament writings?

....

[If you have time: can you think which Old Testament writings Jesus is referring to?

....]

(b) How he faced moral choices

Look up Matthew 4.1–11.

What phrase shows that Jesus took his guidelines for how to live from the Old Testament scriptures?

....

[If you have time: which verses show that Jesus had to know and understand the Old Testament particularly well in order to overcome temptations?

Verses ....]

How *not* to handle the Bible with the unconvinced!

A   is an ordinary, sensible, friendly, nice, open, not-yet-Christian person.

B   is an earnest, zealous, insensitive, but clued-up Christian.

A: (*Yawns*) I am tired.

B: That's because you're spiritually dead. You are one of the sheep that have gone astray, referred to by Jeremiah.

A: I'm not a sheep!

B: (*thinking about this*) No, you're quite right! You are in fact a goat.

A: (*indignant*) I am not!

B: Yes, and the sheep and the goats will be separated at the Seat of Judgement, referred to in Matthew 25.

A: I don't understand all this waffle about sheep and goats. And I certainly don't care about your so-called Seat of Judgement.

B: (*earnestly*) But you are in grave peril because you are unregenerate. You need a new heart, er – Ezekiel thirty-something . . .

A: There's nothing wrong with my heart. It's never stopped! At least, I don't think it has. (*Feels chest anxiously for heartbeat.*)

B: That is a typical red herring, which I shall ignore. Instead I shall tell you that you must repent (Acts 2.38); believe (John 1.12); and accept salvation (Romans 6.23).

A: Look, I just don't believe all this stuff about repenting and having a heart transplant. How do you know it's all true anyway? And what's it got to do with me and my money crisis?

B: These aren't the questions you ought to be asking. You should have asked, "What must I do to be saved?" (Philippian jailer, Acts 16).

A: (*very resigned voice*) OK. "What must I do to be saved, Philippian jailer, Acts 16?"

B: (*completely misunderstanding*) Ah! *Now* you are seriously seeking. You will find the answer in the Bible. Here, I'll lend you mine. (*Hands over vast, old-fashioned tome.*)

Adapted from a script composed and used by generations of Scripture Union staff in England and Wales.

The New Testament rules OK!
Why do Christians believe that the New Testament
carries God's authority as much as the Old does?

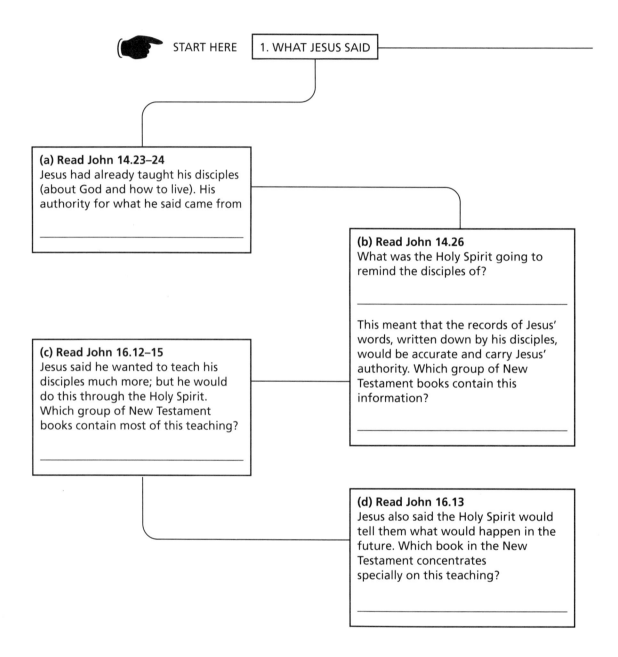

START HERE

1. WHAT JESUS SAID

(a) Read John 14.23–24
Jesus had already taught his disciples
(about God and how to live). His
authority for what he said came from

_____

(b) Read John 14.26
What was the Holy Spirit going to
remind the disciples of?

_____

This meant that the records of Jesus'
words, written down by his disciples,
would be accurate and carry Jesus'
authority. Which group of New
Testament books contain this
information?

_____

(c) Read John 16.12–15
Jesus said he wanted to teach his
disciples much more; but he would
do this through the Holy Spirit.
Which group of New Testament
books contain most of this teaching?

_____

(d) Read John 16.13
Jesus also said the Holy Spirit would
tell them what would happen in the
future. Which book in the New
Testament concentrates
specially on this teaching?

_____

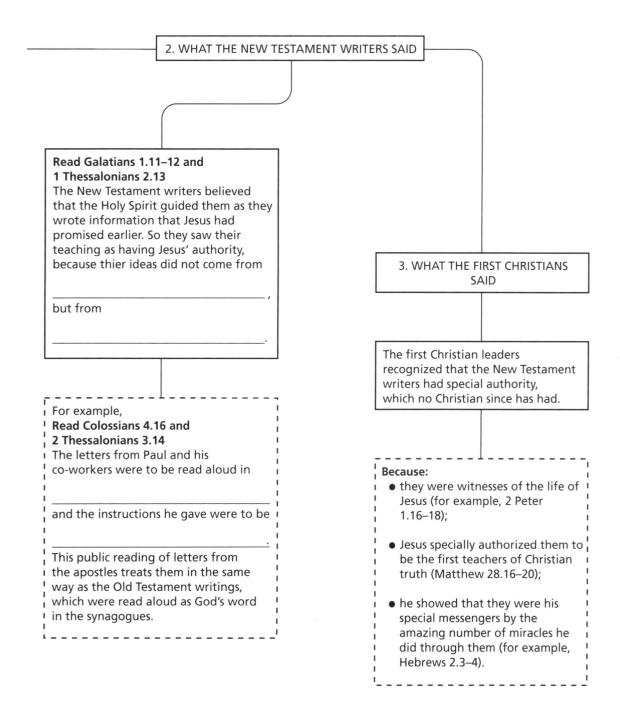

2. WHAT THE NEW TESTAMENT WRITERS SAID

**Read Galatians 1.11–12 and
1 Thessalonians 2.13**
The New Testament writers believed that the Holy Spirit guided them as they wrote information that Jesus had promised earlier. So they saw their teaching as having Jesus' authority, because thier ideas did not come from

_____ ,

but from

_____ .

For example,
**Read Colossians 4.16 and
2 Thessalonians 3.14**
The letters from Paul and his co-workers were to be read aloud in

_____

and the instructions he gave were to be

_____ .

This public reading of letters from the apostles treats them in the same way as the Old Testament writings, which were read aloud as God's word in the synagogues.

3. WHAT THE FIRST CHRISTIANS SAID

The first Christian leaders recognized that the New Testament writers had special authority, which no Christian since has had.

Because:
- they were witnesses of the life of Jesus (for example, 2 Peter 1.16–18);

- Jesus specially authorized them to be the first teachers of Christian truth (Matthew 28.16–20);

- he showed that they were his special messengers by the amazing number of miracles he did through them (for example, Hebrews 2.3–4).

■ SESSION 3

The Bible

BLOCK 2: INFORMATION FOR ENQUIRERS

■ Objections to the Bible

HELPFUL HINTS FOR OBJECTORS
Only use these ideas if you get stuck or find them helpful. Other ideas of your own will be better.

(a)　But it was all written down long after!

Point out that the gospels were probably written as the eyewitnesses of Jesus' life began to die out. Most scholars think Mark's Gospel was the earliest , but he may well not have written it till Peter died in the mid–60s AD, i.e. thirty years after Jesus' death. In thirty years people's memories can get very hazy!

(b)　But what about all the contradictions?

If you know any apparent contradictions in the Bible, mention them. But if you don't, try these:
 (i) The God of the Old Testament is different from the God of the New Testament: in the Old he is always punishing people and causing wars; in the New he is much more loving and forgiving.
 (ii) The Gospels all say different things: one says Jesus healed one blind man, another says two; one has him clearing the temple at the beginning of his ministry, another at the end.

(c)　In the twentieth century it's impossible to believe in the Bible "miracles"!

People were primitive in the first century. When they didn't understand something, they thought it was demon-possession or a miracle. Nowadays we usually know the explanation. Take, for example, the "feeding of the 5,000". Jesus didn't really multiply five loaves and two fishes into a beanfeast. What happened was that when the boy offered to share his rations, everyone else stopped being selfish and got out their bread and meat as well.

(d)　But the gospel writers were biased!

The people who wrote the gospels were "paid-up" Christians, so they were bound to give Jesus a "good press".

　　　　　　　For **Ready to Serve** course use only © Bible Society 1995

- Perhaps they made up the miracles, to get people to listen to them.
- Perhaps they whitewashed Jesus, to make it seem he should never have been crucified.
- Perhaps they dreamed up the resurrection, and especially Jesus' prophecies that he would come back to life, as a sort of wish-fulfilment.

(e)　But hasn't it all been disproved?

You could attack the Bible along the lines of:
  (i) Science – Surely it has disproved belief in creation, miracles, etc.?
  (ii) Archaeology – There are often archaeology programmes on TV showing that all the Bible stories are muddled up and couldn't have happened when and where they say. For example, there's no evidence under the earth's surface of Noah's flood.

HELPFUL HINTS FOR DEFENDERS
Only use these ideas if you get stuck or find them helpful. Other ideas of your own will be better.

(a1)　But it was all written down long after!

- The New Testament story *wasn't* all written down long after! Luke says (1.1) that *many* people had already drawn up accounts of Jesus' life and teaching, before he wrote his gospel. In 1 Corinthians 15.3–5 Paul quotes the "creed" version of Jesus' death and resurrection that he was taught when he first became a Christian – probably only one or two years after the events happened.
- The disciples were preaching and teaching the gospel stories constantly from the day of Pentecost onwards. Something you talk about virtually every day sticks firmly in your mind.
- Before print was invented, people relied much more than we do on passing history down from generation to generation by word of mouth. They revered the truth, and took great care not to distort it. They became used to memorizing important teaching word for word.

(b1)　But what about all the contradictions?

- Try asking, "Like what for instance ....?" Often they don't know any. But usually there is one seeming contradiction in their mind. If you can, try to answer it.
- If you can't, you could say something along the lines of, "Now that I actually read the Bible quite a bit, I can say I've never yet found any real contradictions. There must be an answer to this one, and I'll try to find out what it is."
- Possible answers to two apparent contradictions:

(i) "God is different in the Old and New Testaments." Only in the sense that you have to wait till the New Testament for God's solution to the great problem in the Old Testament: the problem is human guilt and God solves it through Jesus' death. God is both loving and pure throughout the Bible. The OT contains some of the strongest declarations of God's love (for example, "The Lord is my shepherd"); while Jesus in the New Testament gives much more frightening teaching about hell than anything in the Old Testament.

(ii) "The Gospels all say different things." Remember – "different" doesn't necessarily mean they contradict each other. Story-tellers usually focus on *part* of what happened, the memory of one particular eyewitness, not the whole story. What sounds like two conflicting versions of one event may well be reports of two separate events.

(c1) In the twentieth century it's impossible to believe in the Bible miracles!

- Try not to get side-tracked into detailed arguments about modern miracles. It's the miracles in the Bible that we're talking about.
- Miracles don't take up much of the Bible as a whole. But it *does* claim that Jesus performed them repeatedly. If Jesus really *is* God come to earth, this is not surprising. It would be much more unbelievable if he did not perform miracles. So the key question is not "Did the miracles happen?" It is: "Is Jesus God in human form, or just a man?"
- Some of the modern so-called "explanations" of Jesus' miracles treat the gospel writers as naive and even dishonest. Some accuse them of attributing all incurable illnesses to evil spirits, but they drew a distinction between disease and demon-possession (Matthew 4.23–24). And it is quite clear that all the eyewitnesses, not just Jesus' friends, thought they had experienced genuine miracles (for example, John 9.13–16).

(d1) But the gospel writers were biased!

Of course the disciples loved and worshipped Jesus, but they didn't twist the facts. How could they, when Jesus' enemies were all around to dispute any false reports? They were transparently honest. For example,

- they didn't leave out the things they'd rather Jesus hadn't said, for example, that he didn't know when he would come back to earth (Mark 13.32).
- they didn't put in things they'd like Jesus to say. For example, the early Church ran into difficulties over whether Gentiles (i.e. non-Jews) had to become Jews as well as Christians. It would have been very helpful if Jesus had given some teaching on the subject. But Jesus said nothing about it, and they did not make anything up to "put into his mouth".

(e1) But hasn't it all been disproved?

The objector will probably attack along the lines of:

(i) Science: It might be worth pointing out that the Bible is not a science textbook. For example, the early chapters of Genesis are not interested in the scientific details of *how* the world was made, but much more in the relationship between God and his appointed stewards of the world he created.

(ii) Archaeology: Here it is worth knowing that many archaeological discoveries confirm that the Bible is reliable. Two examples:

- The Dead Sea Scrolls (found in 1947) contain copies of parts of the Old Testament 1,000 years older than any previous copies. They are virtually the same as the later versions, and show that the writers who copied the books did not change them.
- In 1888 archaeologists discovered the Pool of Bethzatha in Jerusalem (mentioned in John 5). Previously scholars had suggested that it never existed.

It is not reasonable to expect more than a tiny fraction of the people and events of ancient civilizations to leave archaeological remains. What traces of them would you expect to be found? (If the objectors say that they would expect an event as big as Noah's flood to leave traces, it may be worth pointing out that it may have been a smaller, more local flood than people imagine. When Genesis says that "the rain fell on the *earth*" (7.12), the word it uses can also mean *land,* as in a country (e.g. Eng*land*) or even a district (e.g. Northumber*land*). Also, there are other ancient stories (from outside the Bible) of a flood in the area where early Bible events are said to have taken place, suggesting that it really did happen.)

■ **Session 4** ■

Church

AIM

As with the rest of this series, this session does not seek to look at everything the New Testament teaches about the Church. It tries to relate the parts of New Testament teaching relevant to the practical concerns and questions of new Christians and enquirers. This will equip course members to help these two groups of people more effectively.

BLOCK 1: MY CHURCH – RIGHT OR WRONG

LEADER'S NOTES

Block 1 focuses on your church's ministry to new Christians and outsiders interested in becoming Christians.

1. What would you miss most?

Discussion   5 mins

Form groups of four or five. When everyone is settled, announce that the Martians have landed, taken over control and declared all church meetings illegal. The groups should share what they would find most difficult if they could only talk about Christianity in the privacy of their own homes and families.

After 3 or 4 minutes, hear a few thoughts from one or two of the groups. Draw the conclusion that it is impossible to be a Christian all on one's own, we cannot function in isolation.

2. Is our church worth joining?

Questionnaire   15 mins

Give everyone a copy of pages 41–44. They should work through the questionnaire for about 10 minutes, alone or in the same small groups. Tell them that the Bible blueprint is Acts 2.41–42. This is far more important than the detailed suggestions in the questionnaire, which are *only* suggestions. They are free to disagree with them, and improve on them when you discuss them together later.

Share your thoughts as a full course for 5 minutes. If anything emerges as "a good idea for us to try", be ready to pass it on to the relevant leadership body in your church.

3. No church is perfect!

Buzz-groups   15 mins

It is highly unlikely that any of your course members think your church is perfect! But it is easy to become complacent, and lose sight of how we appear to new Christians and to outsiders. For instance, almost all church members think *their* church is very friendly, but that is not always the impression that newcomers receive.

Move people onto the next activity. Divide into groups of three or four, with someone in each group who is a fairly recent new Christian or newcomer to your church. The groups should think of any weaknesses or gaps in your church's ministry to the target-group we are always focusing on in this series: new Christians and friends who are not Christians. But for each weakness, they must think of some positive action they could take; prayer would count as a *very* positive form of action.

They should move on to spend the second 5 minutes turning one of their actions into a definite suggestion.

In the last 5 minutes hear each group's suggestion. To keep the reporting back quick and crisp, say:

"Don't explain, don't apologize, just read."

It will help if you write up their recommendations on a board or OHP. Again offer to pass ideas on to your church's leadership.

4. Pass the cup

Express-your-feelings exercise   10 mins

You may want to spend the rest of the block *discussing* people's ideas and feelings. Alternatively, do this expressive exercise. It only works really well when the course members have come to know each other well enough to feel relaxed together and committed to each other.

Join the small groups together into one or more circles with a maximum of ten in each. Supply an unused disposable coffee cup for each person; cardboard cups are ideal, but if you can only get plastic or polystyrene, supply a pair of scissors or sharp knife to each circle! Also supply some coloured pens. Tell people that the cup represents "our church fellowship". Ask people to think how they could express without words how they see "our church", or what they would like to do to it. (It might be anything from kissing it, decorating it, or bandaging it, to ripping it open, spitting on it, or setting it on fire – mime or real!). Encourage them to think not only of their own feelings, but of how the church must appear to new Christians and outsiders in the area.

If it involves colouring or decoration, tell them to do it during these few minutes while people are thinking; if it is a quicker action, tell them to wait!

When everyone is ready, each should take it in turn to show their cup to the rest of their circle, and either pour their feelings into it or take their feelings out on it.

Carry on round the circle without comment till everyone has had a turn. Then break the silence and discuss what you did. People may have expressed powerful feelings, which they will now need time (and sympathetic listeners) to explain. Ask people to try to listen without shock, and certainly without arguing. Perhaps break back down into smaller groups.

BLOCK 2: THE IDENTIKIT CHURCH MEMBER

Block 2 focuses on what is involved in being a church member, first for new Christians, then by way of a check-up for course members.

1. Why do you go to church?

Role play   5 mins

Form groups of two or three (not more) by partnering people with the one or two beside them. One of them is to play the part of a young teenager, the other one or two are just themselves. Hold a conversation where the teenager asks (and wants a good answer!), "Surely you don't have to go to church to be a Christian?" If your course members have done the Advanced Level home assignment, they should use their preparation.

At the end, ask people to share answers that seemed particularly effective.

2. The identikit church member

Drama and discussion   25 mins

To explore the responsibilities of church membership, ask two suitable members of the course (ideally with drama experience) to prepare in advance and now perform an interview between a church minister and a new member just joining up (for example, according to your tradition, coming to confirmation, baptism or reception into membership, etc.)

The minister stresses that the new member now has a loyalty in four areas:

(a) The central meeting of the church – certainly the Sunday service, but perhaps a mid-week fellowship as well. He or she quotes Hebrews 10.25.

(b) A small home fellowship group – a mid-week subdivision of the church that meets for Bible study and prayer. He or she quotes Matthew 18.20.

(c) Practical Christian service – the minister probably has some job in mind that the new member would be "just the right person" to do. He or she quotes 1 Corinthians 12.7.

(d) Regular, committed giving of money – the minister suggests a target amount or percentage. He or she quotes 1 Corinthians 16.2.

The more amusing you can make this, while still making the points clear, the better. Therefore it may be better if the real minister does not play the minister, but someone else who makes use of some of the real minister's favourite phrases and gestures. Adapt the details to local custom. If, for example, your church holds no small home groups, still make point (b), but in respect of an informal prayer cell. The new member should resist on some points (e.g. "Not free that night", "But I'd rather just arrange the flowers", "I don't think I could give that much money", etc.), but not unreasonably; remember, he or she *is* a new member!

After the sketch, the small groups from activity 1 should discuss the points together and consider the Bible passages, with the help of page 46 in the members' pages. Which order of importance would they put these commitments in?

Take 3 or 4 minutes at the end to hear answers and reasons from a few groups.

3. How can I fit it all in?

Personal check-up

15 mins

It is all very well giving advice to new Christians; but we must not duck the challenge to ourselves. When we think about how much of ourselves we could and should contribute to our church, we feel the conflicting calls on our time: family, work, community involvement, etc. All vie with church. It is good to take stock regularly of our life-pattern.

People should work on their own on the personal check-up on pages 46–47. Perhaps round things off with a few moments' silence, and then say the Grace or Lord's Prayer together. Announce that you are available (now or at another time) to talk with anyone who would like further help in thinking their commitments through.

LEADER'S NOTES

SESSION 4

Church

BLOCK 1: MY CHURCH – RIGHT OR WRONG

■ Is our church worth joining?

This is a check-list to test how healthy your church is for attracting outsiders and helping new Christians to grow in their faith.

Here is Luke's description of the first church:

> Many of them believed his [Peter's] message and were baptized, and about three thousand people were added to the group that day. They spent their time in learning from the apostles, taking part in the fellowship, and sharing in the fellowship meals and the prayers (Acts 2.41–42).

It is a good pattern for any church to follow. So answer these questions (tick for YES, cross for NO, question mark for SOMETIMES) to see how your church scores.

(a) The apostles' teaching

This is available today through the books the apostles wrote and taught from, i.e. the Bible. This is the source of the Good News that outsiders need to hear, and it is the spiritual food new Christians need to feed on.

(1) In Sunday services:
  (a) Is everyone given, or asked to bring, a Bible to refer to?
  (b) Are the readings from a translation of the Bible that is easy for people new to the faith to understand?
  (c) Are the readings shown to be important by having good readers who obviously prepare and practise their readings, and take the trouble to read clearly?
  (d) Are there attempts sometimes to make the reading more "alive" (e.g. by having different readers for different characters, or adding movement or music)?
  (e) Do any of the songs and prayers follow the theme of the readings?
  (f) Does the teaching follow the theme of the readings?
  (g) Is the teaching clearly based on the Bible?
  (h) Does the teaching usually use some other educational aid, suited to the age-range (for example, overhead projector, handout sheets, pictures, puppets, etc.) to make the teaching clearer?
  (i) Is there any attempt after the teaching to check whether you are putting it into practice (perhaps by having questions, group discussion, further reading, a quiz the following week)?

(2) In mid-week fellowship:

  (a) Is there at least one group meeting to study the Bible?

  (b) Does the discussion try to learn from the Bible and stay close to the subject?

  (c) Does it lead into a time of prayer when the group asks God's help to live out what they've learnt?

  (d) Have you noticed any members of the group change their behaviour as a result of what they learn from the Bible?

(b) Taking part in the fellowship

This suggests deeply committed friendships and caring action. These are a vital climate for helping people grow closer to God.

(1) Friendship:

  (a) Are there at least some people on the lookout at every Sunday service to welcome newcomers, and particularly any who may not yet be Christians?

  (b) Are most of the conversations you overhear on a Sunday helpful, loving and thoughtful, rather than purely superficial?

  (c) Are there frequent social events at which people can get to know each other in an enjoyable, relaxed setting?

  (d) Do church members regularly invite new Christians and those who are not Christians into their homes?

  (e) Do more than half your members clearly treat church membership as their top priority after their closest family?

  (f) Does your church magazine or news-sheet feature news of what members have been up to?

  (g) Is it clear every week that children and teenagers are as much part of the church family as adults are?

(2) Action:

  (a) Does your church provide a list of members' names, addresses and telephone numbers for each member to use?

  (b) Are more than half of your members clearly known to have at least one responsibility in the work of the church (for example, choir, children's teacher, magazine distributor, home-group leader)?

  (c) Is there a regular programme of visiting newcomers to the area and people with only a slight connection with the church, by more than just the full-time staff?

  (d) Is there a regular programme of visiting old people and those in hospital by more than just the full-time staff?

  (e) Is there an effective system of caring for new Christians and those with problems?

(c) Fellowship meals

This refers supremely to celebrating "the Lord's Supper" or "Holy Communion" (or whatever name your church uses).

The vivid demonstration of Jesus' body broken and blood shed on the cross is another powerful way in which God makes himself known to us. By receiving the bread and wine in communion, we celebrate the death and resurrection of Jesus – which is at the heart of the Good News – as well as demonstrating our openness to our relationship with God through Jesus Christ.

(a) Is this celebration *central* in your church's pattern of services, i.e. regular, frequent, shown to be important, welcoming to the majority of attenders?

(b) Do you regularly give guidance to new, young Christians on how to understand and make the most of the service?

(c) Do you make it clear, on the other hand, that people should not take part with a flippant or unworthy attitude? In particular, do you help any present who are not Christians understand what is going on?

(d) Do your service-leaders help you to use the silences and pauses in this service well (for example, by giving suggested topics for prayer, or a music group playing or singing)?

(d) Prayer

This refers primarily to the church's united praying in services and other meetings, but naturally spills over to influence personal prayer as well.

(a) Are there attempts to make the prayer times in your services more meaningful (for example, by using words of response for the congregation, by group sharing or other means of people contributing their requests, by having people available to pray with anyone in need after the service)?

(b) Does your church hold gatherings exclusively for prayer (i.e. business or Bible discussions not included!), whether small or large, regularly or for special occasions?

(c) Do outreach to outsiders and care for new Christians appear to be major prayer concerns of your church?

(d) Do your church business meetings include unhurried time for prayer?

(e) Can you remember receiving teaching from your church during the last year on how to pray more effectively?

(f) Does your church produce some form of prayer diary to encourage regular prayer for the members?

Now add up the ticks to see how many points your church scores out of 35, question marks count as half a point.

TOTAL

_____

31–35:   Lucky you! Do you appreciate how true your church is seeking to be to the Bible's blueprint?

26–30:   Your church has a great deal to pass on, both to other churches and to outsiders in your area. Have you ever thought what you should be doing to share these ideas and approaches with others?

16–25:   Can you see areas of need in your church's life which you could work on building up?

0–15 :   Is it really the church, or is it perhaps you, who lags so far behind the New Testament? Or didn't you have time to finish the list?!

No church is perfect!

Even if you gave your church a high score in the check-list, it is not perfect. Think now of your weaknesses as a church, especially in your service to new Christians and to those you are trying to share the Good News with. Write them in the left-hand column below.

For each weakness, put at least one action in the right column which could improve matters. If you can think of an action you yourself could help with, so much the better.

WEAKNESS   ACTION

(1) ....   (1) ....

    ....

(2) ....   (2) ....

    ....

(3) ....   (3) ....

    ....

(4) ....   (4) ....

    ....

(5) ....   (5) ....

    ....

SUGGESTION

With the rest of your group, select one weakness and one piece of action to deal with it. Write it up as a recommendation for your church to act on.

We feel that an important way for our church to do its job of caring for new Christians and reaching outsiders better is to:

....

....

....

....

....

....

....

....

After a few minutes, you will be asked to read out your suggestion.

Church

BLOCK 2: THE IDENTIKIT CHURCH MEMBER

■ The identikit church member

Church commitments:
Central meeting
Small group
Practical Christian service
Giving money

Bible passages:
Hebrews 10.25
Matthew 18.20
1 Corinthians 12.7
1 Corinthians 16.2

How would you rate these church commitments in order of importance for a new Christian?

(1) ....

(2) ....

(3) ....

(4) ....

■ How can I fit it all in?

It is all very well giving advice to new church members. But what sort of example am I? In this personal check-up, be thoroughly realistic.

Look up 1 Timothy 5.4–8.
What does Paul mean that my duty as a family member should be?

....

....

Look up Ephesians 6.5–9
If I am in paid employment, what does Paul mean that my duty as an employee or employer should be? (NB *Obviously* relationships in twentieth-century workplaces are different from first-century slaves and masters – at least we hope so! But what underlying attitudes and truths in these verses remain important for us today?)

....

....

Look up Mark 6.30–32.
What does Jesus mean that my duty to my own health should be?

....

....

Look up John 13.1–17, 34–35.
What does Jesus mean my duty to fellow-Christians to be?

....

....

Look up John 17.13–21.
What does Jesus mean for my duty to those who are not Christians to be?

....

....

HOW DO I FIT IT ALL IN?
In an average week, how much
time do you spend in each of
these five areas:

HOW CAN I FIT IT IN BETTER?
Assuming the present
arrangement is not
perfect, what would be a
better (but still possible)
balance of time available?

FAMILY   ....

WORK   ....

REST   ....

CHURCH   ....

NON-CHRISTIAN
FRIENDS   ....

In order to reach a better balance of my time, I should make the following
changes *during the next week!*

....

....

....

....

....

■ **Session 5** ■

Doubts, suffering and guidance

AIM

This session looks at some common problems that worry new Christians and those considering the faith from outside the church. Block 1 focuses on some of the doubts that many new Christians go through. Block 2 takes two other common areas of doubt: suffering (often a major stumbling-block for those who are not Christians) and guidance (often a big worry to new Christians). This is a huge subject-area and could well spread out into two sessions if you have time.

Although our focus is on equipping course members to help others, many of them will have their own pain and problems in this subject area. It is probably wise to tell them at the beginning that they can sit out of any activity if it feels uncomfortable, and that you will be available afterwards to talk to anyone who is upset. Alert any gifted carers on the course to be ready to help. It might also be worth offering general or private discussion of any areas of doubt which the session does not cover.

BLOCK 1: DOUBTS

1. How can you be so sure?

Short talk   5 mins

Ask the course how many of them have had friends ask, "How can you be so sure you're right about Christianity?" Ask one or two to explain (briefly) how they answered the question.

Then put the following statement into your own words and present at least the three headings visually:

It is possible to be sure that you are a Christian, because the Bible provides a strong three-point basis for our faith:

(a) Jesus' promises, for example, John 6 (particularly verse 37). We can rely on Jesus to keep his promises.

(b) Jesus' death, for example, 1 Peter 3. 18 to the end. Jesus died on the cross "once for all"; that one act of self-giving was enough to pay for all the sins of all human beings, past, present and future. The fact that he then came back to life proves that there was no further debt to pay.

(c) Jesus' Spirit, for example, Romans 8 (particularly verses 15 and 16). The Holy Spirit helps us to *know*, each in our own way, that God is our Father.

2. Stale-patch Stella

Sharing, study and prayer   20 mins

Now divide people into pairs who would naturally share confidences together, and give them a copy of members' pages 51–52. They should spend 5 minutes on item (a), 10 minutes on (b), and 5 minutes on (c).

Break in at the appropriate moments to move them on to the next item. It does not matter if they have not finished the previous question; they should go on to the next at once.

3. Does God still love me?

Case studies and discussion   20 mins

Some people are particularly prone to feeling "God doesn't care about me", because of aspects of their character or background. This activity looks at three common examples: unhappy family, guilt feelings and stress. They may well be common among the friends of course members.

One good way to introduce a five-minute general discussion on how to understand and help people with each of the three problems, would be to use:

(i) **Tableau sculptures** You take the required number of people and group them so that they are "frozen" like statues in positions that explain the central character's self-doubt. Tell them to take special care over gestures, facial expressions, etc., or (more fun) silently mould their arms, legs, faces, etc., yourself as if you were a sculptor.

(ii) **Bible readings** When you have set up the tableau, and explained it to the "audience", ask someone to read a short passage from the Bible that reassures or "speaks to" the self-doubt. The tableau actors should stay in position.

Here are the suggested characters and Bible passages:

(a) Unhappy Family Background

Show: * A small person, perhaps kneeling, to represent a child, with a label round the neck which reads, "Nobody cares about me, so why should God?"

* Father turning to leave the house after a furious row with mother.

* Mother taking out her feelings by slapping the child.

Read: Psalm 27.8–10 and Matthew 7.7–11.

(b) Guilt Feelings

Show: * Someone looking very guilty, with a label round their neck which reads, "God will never forgive me";

* Four characters surrounding and accusing this person. They are labelled "Pride", "Envy", "Hate" and "Greed", and should look the part with their faces. They represent the thoughts of the first person.

Read: l John 1.9 and Romans 8.31–34.

(c) Stress

Show: * A business person in an office with vast pile of papers to see to, with a label round the neck which reads, "Why does God allow all this to fall on me?"

* demanding boss;

* bitter, neglected spouse and rebellious teenage children.

Read: 1 Kings 19.3–8 and Isaiah 40.27–31.

However you introduce the characters, lead a short discussion on each, making sure that you cover the questions:

(i) In what ways is Christian discipleship made harder for such a person?

(ii) How does the Bible's teaching help them?

(iii) How can *we* help them?

Encourage people to note any good suggestions.

In dealing with (b) Guilt Feelings, you need to make sure that people understand the difference between real guilt and an unhealthy over-awareness of sin. God is holy; he banishes sin, and took ultimate steps to deal with it by dying for us on the cross. As Christians, we can therefore experience his forgiveness for our guilt and freedom from it. But some Christians go on feeling morbidly guilty, even after they have confessed their sin and been assured of God's forgiveness.

Give them a few moments at the end to reflect on *who* they could help as a result of this block and *how* they might do it.

BLOCK 2: SUFFERING AND GUIDANCE

1. That really hurt!

Sharing

5 mins

Ask people, in pairs, to reflect for a moment and then share a painful experience they have had, and which they feel able to talk about. Guide them and reassure them with words such as: "The pain may have been physical, mental or emotional; it may have been only for a day or two, or have lasted for years. It may now seem trivial or still horrific. But your partner will respect what was for you a painful experience by listening carefully and being sympathetic.

You don't need to go into lots of detail; just say enough to help your partner understand what happened and how you felt." Make sure that people know that whatever they share will not go beyond the confines of this group.

2. A shoulder to cry on

Brainstorm

5 mins

Ask everyone what advice they would give for being a helpful friend or counsellor to someone in distress. Make this a "brainstorm", i.e. a general pooling of ideas. You could set the ball rolling by asking, for instance, "What did *you* find helpful when suffering the painful experience you have just been talking about?" The golden rule of a brainstorm is that you are only allowed to *give* ideas or tips, *not* to comment on anyone else's. This means that all suggestions, even the most simple and obvious, are welcome. But ask people to keep them short. Write them up on a board or an OHP.

Let the brainstorm run for 2 to 3 minutes maximum. Then give people a chance to note any of the ideas they like. As they do so, let people comment on any specially helpful ideas that have come up. But no-one should criticize or disagree with what has been helpful to someone else.

3. Words of understanding, words of comfort

Bible study   15 mins

Move on to the next activity on pages 54–56, a study of 2 Corinthians 1.3–11, which everyone should work through at their own pace. This will add Paul and Timothy's experience to the brainstorm ideas. Ask people to work either alone or with the same person as before.

The "imaginative" exercises in the first two sections may seem a distraction to "serious" Bible students and are not essential; but they are an attempt to help people *feel* and express the emotions behind the words, as a more complete response to the passage. Have some coloured pens available for people who want to use them.

Break in to suggest that everybody considers the final question for the last 3 minutes at least.

4. Why doesn't God just tell me what to do?

Flow chart   20 mins

Join together pairs from earlier in the block to form groups of four who are likely to work well together. Perhaps introduce the subject of guidance yourself by reading one of God's promises to guide, for example, Psalm 32.8–9. Ask one person in each group of four to offer to be the centre of discussion. Ideally she or he should be someone who is seeking God's guidance at the moment about some major decision (perhaps changing job, moving house, taking on a new commitment at church). If there is nobody in that position, they should focus on someone who has recently been through the experience.

Members' pages 56–57 map out a suggested step-by-step process for discovering God's will, although the different stages may occur in any order, or all at once! Work through them in the groups, seeing if they help (or helped) your guinea-pig. When they reach a "Wait", they should still explore the other steps. If they reach a "Stop", they should ask one of the other members to have a go.

Finish by asking or thanking God together for his clear guidance. Pray for any members of the course who need God's leading at the moment; but also for any of their Christian friends. Encourage them to think how they might pass on anything they have learnt in this session.

SESSION 5

Doubts, suffering and guidance

BLOCK 1: DOUBTS

■ Stale-patch Stella

Stella has been a happy, healthy Christian for as long as you can remember. But just recently she appears perplexed and unsmiling. When you ask her "What's up?", she says, "I can't understand it, but everything's gone dead. Being a Christian doesn't seem as real as it used to."

(a) With your working partner, share any spiritual "dry patches" that you have experienced or may be experiencing now. What do they feel like? How do they affect you? What difference do they make?

(b) Look together at Psalm 42. Read it aloud, one of you verses 1 to 5, the other verses 6 to 11. Then try together to answer the following questions about it.

 (i) Read the following statement. If you think it is true, put a T in the circle; if false, put an F in the circle.

 This psalm shows that "spiritual dryness" (or feeling far away from God) should never happen to God's people.

 Which verses would you choose to support or contradict the statement?

 Verse(s) ....

 (ii) Complete this statement:
 According to verse 4, spiritual dryness is all the harder, because nothing

 feels so ....

 as it did in the ....

 (iii) What seem to have been the reasons for the writer's dry patch?

 ....

 ....

 ....

What might be some reasons for Christians having dry patches today?

....

....

(iv) Rewrite verses 1 and 2 in your own words, so that they express a good resolution (which need not come at the New Year) for the next time you hit a dry patch:

....

....

....

Discuss how you would advise Stale-patch Stella when she says: "I'm not getting anything out of church services any more, so I'm going to stop coming."

(v) Think of one word to describe the psalm-writer's mood in his "refrain" at the end of verses 5 and 11:

....

(c) If you have not had time to look at question b(v), answer it now. With your working partner, share what you think God wants you to learn or remember *now* from this psalm; either for your own benefit, or to pass on to anyone you know who is like Stella in some way. Silently or aloud, spend a few moments praying for the person you have been working with or the person they are concerned for.

■ Does God still love me?

How to help people with doubts caused by:

(a) UNHAPPY FAMILY BACKGROUND

(b) GUILT FEELINGS

(c) STRESS

Is there someone you know who has one or more of the problems covered in this session? ....

How might you be able to help them?

....

....

SESSION 5

Doubts, suffering and guidance

BLOCK 2: SUFFERING AND GUIDANCE

■ A shoulder to cry on

> HOW TO BE A HELPFUL FRIEND OR COUNSELLOR TO SOMEONE IN DISTRESS.
> (Note any good ideas from your brainstorm.)

■ Words of understanding, words of comfort

> Look up 2 Corinthians 1.3–11, and study it with these questions, alone or with someone else.

A load of trouble (verses 8–10)

> Pick out three or four words from these verses, which show that Paul and Timothy (the "we" who are speaking in the letter) suffered very heavily:
>
> ....
>
> They do not tell us exactly what they were suffering from. What do you imagine it might have been?
>
> ....

Draw two shapes to represent Paul and Timothy's troubles on one side, yours on the other (either your present difficulties, or the painful experience you discussed earlier). Let the shapes express your feelings about the suffering, as you experienced it and Paul and Timothy described it:

Paul and Timothy's troubles   My troubles

The silver lining (verses 3–7)

In column (a), write down three thoughts from these verses which bring comfort, and help you to see some good in suffering:

(a)   **(b)**

(i) ....   (i) ....

(ii) ....   (ii) ....

(iii) ....   (iii) ....

In column (b), write the name of someone you know who you could help by sharing this thought with them. It might be the same person each time, but not necessarily.

   What colour or colours do you associate with "the sufferings of Christ" (verse 5) in their different forms? (Use this space to draw a splash of colours, if that expresses your feelings better than a list of words.)

A very present help (verses 9–11)

From these verses, note:

(a) a way that sufferers can help themselves:

....

(b) a way that their friends can help them:

....

What have you learnt about suffering and comfort from this session?

....

....

What do you think God might be asking you to do as a result of it? (For example, is there someone you might be able to help?)

....

....

■ Why doesn't God just tell me what to do?

A flow chart for discovering where God is leading you

Read each Bible passage, and the question that flows from it. Answer the question as far as you can. Does the recommended action on the flow chart seem the best step to take?

(a) BIBLE

Joshua 1.1–8 Does the course of action you are considering conflict with the guidelines for living that God has laid down in the Bible?

STOP! ← YES   NO
                                                                                  ↓
                                                                              Proceed

---

(b) THOUGHT

Romans 12.1–2 Does it "grow on you", the more you find out about it and think it over from God's point of view?

YES   NO → Wait
↓
Proceed

(c) PRAYER AND PEACE

Romans 8.5–8, 12–16 As you pray about it and ask God to guide your decision, is your state of mind increasingly one of settled peace?

YES   NO → Wait
↓
Proceed

For **Ready to Serve** course use only © Bible Society 1995

(d) ADVICE

Proverbs 15.22 Do those who know you best think it is a good move?

YES   NO → Wait
↓

Proceed

(e) CIRCUMSTANCES

Romans 8.28–30 Are there any good side-effects, or more recent indicators, which make it seem a change for the better?

YES   NO → Wait
↓   and reconsider

This sounds very much as if it is the direction that God is leading you in. Proceed with caution: be ready for him even now to take you on a different course. And don't be too disappointed if he does!

■ Session 6 ■

Marriage and singleness

AIM

No aspect of Christian life is under more constant attack than its attitude to sexual relationships and living. This is certainly not the only important ethical issue today – perhaps not even the most important – but it is the one that course members will find themselves talking about most often. It is therefore given a whole session. It is vital that we learn how to explain the Bible's teaching, or new Christians and interested onlookers will believe the widespread propaganda that no-one takes Christian principles seriously any more.

Once again, our focus is on helping others. But it is more than likely that some of your course members have difficulties with this area of life. Remind them that you and, if possible, other gifted carers are available at any time to talk and pray.

LEADER'S NOTES

BLOCK 1: MARRIED OR SINGLE?

1. Find your partner

Party game

5 mins

Compile a list of famous married couples. You could limit yourself to the Bible:

e.g,   Abraham and Sarah
      Aquila and Priscilla

or broaden your scope to cover history, literature, films, etc.

e.g,   Romeo and Juliet
      Scarlet O'Hara and Rhett Butler
      Henry VIII and Anne Boleyn
      Bill and Hilary Clinton

Prepare a slip of paper for each individual name. Give one slip to each member of the group as they arrive. They should then find their partners, and stay with them for the rest of the block. You don't need to have equal numbers of men and women members; it can be fun to give a man's name to a woman, and vice versa.

Refinements if you have time:

(a) Stick the name on people's backs, and ask them to guess who they are by asking other people

questions. When they have guessed, they look for their partners.

(b) It could also be very telling, whether or not your course has an odd number, to include some names of single people: e.g. St Paul, Mother Teresa, Cliff Richard, Elizabeth I, Florence Nightingale; or (perhaps better) some married people's names without their husbands or wives, so that the group member looks unsuccessfully for her or his partner. Ask them at the end of the game how it felt to be "left out".

2. A Christian view of marriage

Bible study

20 mins

Form groups of four or five by putting two pairs (with a "single") together. Give everyone a copy of members' pages 61–63 and work through them together. It is probably better, at first, that they discuss the questions in groups, rather than work alone. Gently move them on to the next question every 5 minutes. It is better to *start* each question, than to complete only one or two.

3. A Christian view of singleness

Bible study and input

 20 mins

The following notes are taken from a conversation between two people; one putting the advantages of singleness from St Paul's viewpoint (A – focused on 1 Corinthians 7), and the other responding to those ideas as a single person today (B). You could either read these notes of St Paul's view, preferably filling them out with examples (real or typical) of people for whom singleness has been an advantage; or prepare your own talk on 1 Corinthians 7. Allow time for people to make their own notes as they listen.

The single person's responses appear in diagram form on members' page 65. Pause to reflect on them after each of the three main points, perhaps asking people to say which they think is the most important difficulty and piece of positive action in each case.

If you have time, it may be helpful to discuss both the biblical points and the responses as a full course; and to ask a member of your church who is single, and happy to talk about it, to compare her or his experiences. However, be aware that if this is discussed at a superficial level it can be hard to accept, so try to make sure that the result of the discussion *is* a deeper appreciation of the Bible's teaching, not an unthinking rejection of it! Or if for the members of your group, the single life is something of a distant memory, it may be necessary to make sure they do not make an equally *unthinking* acceptance of it.

(A) St Paul's view – Notes on 1 Corinthians 7

(1) **Introductory points:**

(a) The passage we have looked at so far is God's creation of marriage in the Old Testament; for the most part, the New Testament takes its teaching on married life straight from the Old Testament. The Old Testament sees no higher estate than a happy marriage, and no greater blessing than having children. So it begins with the command to be fruitful and multiply, and to fill the earth (Genesis 1.26–28).

(b) But the New Testament brings a new era into being with the death and resurrection of Jesus. The greatest happiness in the world now changes: it is no longer to fill the earth, but to

win it; not to have physical children, but spiritual ones. The new era is launched with a new command: to go and make disciples of all nations (Matthew 28.19,20).

(c) The New Testament continues to rejoice in marriage, but no longer sees it as the highest good. For the first time, there is a positive value in singleness. This was a revolutionary view for a Jew of that time.

(d) Many people say that Paul, as a bachelor, was biased in his view of marriage. But it would be more accurate to say that, as a single person who was also an apostle, he was uniquely qualified to speak on the subject – in a way that a married man like Peter was not. Moreover, Paul's teaching corresponds closely to Jesus' reported words (see Matthew 19.10–12).

(e) In this passage Paul draws directly on the teachings of Jesus (verse 10), and on his own understanding where there is no remembered statement of Jesus which is relevant to the specific situation (verse 12). However, even though this is Paul's personal opinion, as an apostle he believes that God is guiding his thoughts (verse 40), and that because of this his teaching carries God's authority (verse 25).

(2) **Main points** – Advantages of being single According to Paul in 1 Corinthians 7:

(a) Singleness as a gift from God (verse 7).
   God plans that some should be married and some single. Neither state is a right to which we have a claim. Paul sees the ability to live a single life as a specific spiritual gift from God. Like other spiritual gifts, it is one which we can set our hearts on and ask God for (1 Corinthians 12–14). Seeing our state from God's perspective, we should try to accept our singleness joyfully and thankfully and use all the possibilities it offers to draw close to God and serve him.

(b) Singleness can free us from earthly ties and worries (verses 25–31).
   Paul, looking at the whole history of the world, sees that the last but one of the great events has taken place (the outpouring of the Spirit at Pentecost). We are therefore in the "last days", which prophets said would be full of trouble, distress and suffering. So the freer one is, the better (see especially verse 28). Where married people, particularly parents with young families,

LEADER'S NOTES

have earthbound ties and responsibilities such as their children's health, upbringing and education, a single person does not have this sort of consideration to take into account when they look at ways to serve God and prepare for life in heaven. Usually this service will be in work or wider family commitments, but it could involve going abroad as a missionary, relief or development worker, or devoting all your time and attention to church or community work.

(c) Singleness can provide the opportunity to give more undivided attention to the Lord and his work (verses 32–35). A married person needs to invest time working at their relationship with their spouse (and possibly family), and consequently probably has less time to devote to their relationship with the Lord. A single person has the opportunity to give some of this time and energy to developing their relationship with the Lord and doing his work.

BLOCK 2: THIS YEAR, NEXT YEAR . . .

1. "Family" role plays

30 mins

Divide people into groups of three or four. They should take on the roles of father, mother and teenage children. All are Christians. They may stick to one role throughout the session, or swap round between conversations. If there is no man in the group, or if the subject seems unrealistic for a family discussion, the two "adults" should instead play the part of leaders of the youth fellowship. These "parents" or "youth leaders" may well be grateful for the guide-passages and suggestions on pages 66–69 in the members' pages, and the chance to look them through before the role play starts; but they should use their own thoughts or knowledge in preference. The conversation begins with the "teenagers" saying one of the opening remarks on page 66; you need to choose which one, probably one that is not too personal to start with.

The best timing is probably 5 minutes of role play, followed by 5 minutes of discussion. It is important to discuss the role play and issues raised. You might ask for quick reports or ideas from the "families" once or twice, and leave them to discuss within their groups the other times.

Thirty minutes should allow you time for three role plays. Select the subjects from the list in the Members' pages, or substitute others of your own. Be sensitive to what is relevant to your course members, and the conversations they are likely to have with younger Christians or friends and family who are not yet Christians. Conversations E and F are most closely connected with the home assignments for this session.

They are all controversial questions. The relationship between the adults and teenagers is a good one, and the teenager(s) should respect their answers; but they may well question the reasons for

them till they are satisfied, and voice their friends' common objections to them. If there is a second "teenager" in the "family", they could ask the question jointly; or the second teenager could help to answer it as a more mature Christian; or object to it more strongly as a less mature Christian! To save time, you as leader could decide this family balance.

Although course members may not all be in a position to talk to teenagers in real life about these issues, they are also a talking point with many adults new to Christian faith or close to it.

2. Questions and discussion

10 mins

The role plays are bound to raise issues that people will want to explore further as a full course. Encourage them to think particularly of what their friends who are younger Christians or outside the church say and think. If you have someone suitable in your church or area, invite them to help you answer questions.

3. Epilogue

5 mins

Read 1 Corinthians 6.9–11 and comment on it in your own words. Note particularly:

(a) God has set standards for our sexuality, as much as for any other area of our lives.

(b) Some of the Corinthians had failed to live up to these standards. Probably all of us have failed, and will continue to do so, to one degree or another.

(c) That is not the end of the story! There is forgiveness, a new start, and progress available for all Christians. This is the great news we bring both to those who are already Christians, and to those who have not yet started.

SESSION 6
Marriage and singleness

BLOCK 1: MARRIED OR SINGLE?

■ A Christian view of marriage

(a) Marriage is a balanced relationship

Read Genesis 2.18–20.
What does God say he designed wives to be?

....

Which of these words seem to you to describe God's plan for married women?

drudgery
"the little woman"
willing submission
partnership
romance
complete independence

God does not say here in so many words what he wants husbands to be like.
But which of these descriptions seem to you best to fit into the sort of
marriage he has in mind?

henpecked
lord and master
suitable companion
breadwinner

Suggest which TV husbands and wives clearly *do not* conform to this pattern,
and any that *do*.

....

....

....

....

....

(b) Marriage is the basic relationship

Read Genesis 2.21–24.

In what ways can a husband or wife *fail* to leave father and mother?

....

....

....

With what results (apart from mother-in-law jokes!)?

....

....

....

Do you think the *minimum* marrying age should be 16 or 18 – or some other age?

....

Do you think there is a *best* age for getting married?

....

(c) Marriage is a unifying relationship

Read again Genesis 2.24.
What does Jesus add to this statement in Mark 10.6–9?

....

....

What do you think he means by this?

....

....

If two people are going to join together to become one unit (flesh), they obviously need to have a lot in common. Tick which of the following you think it is *essential* for them to share. Then grade the rest in order of desirability:

☐ being in love with each other   ☐ similar age

☐ same nationality   ☐ spare-time interests

☐ political views   ☐ intellectual ability

☐ food likes and dislikes   ☐ attitude to children

☐ social background   ☐ respect for each other

☐ religious faith or philosophy of life   ☐ sexual attraction

(d) Marriage is a sexual relationship

Read Genesis 4.1.
The word translated as sexual intercourse is "to know", i.e. sex is at the heart of their relationship and deepens it.

Collect some good answers from the group to these common opinions:

"You don't have to be married to live together or sleep together."

....

....

....

"The Bible is anti-sex."

....

....

....

■ A CHRISTIAN VIEW OF SINGLENESS

(a) St Paul's view (1 Corinthians 7)

(1) Introductory points:

(a)

(b)

(c)

(d)

(e)

(2) Advantages of being single:

(a) A gift from God (verse 7)
Notes:

....

....

....

....

....

(b) Can free us from earthly ties and worries (verses 25–31)
Notes:

....

....

....

....

....

....

(c) Opportunity to give more attention to the Lord and his work (verses 32–35)
Notes:

....

....

....

....

....

....

THE SINGLE PERSON'S EXPERIENCE

(a) A gift from God

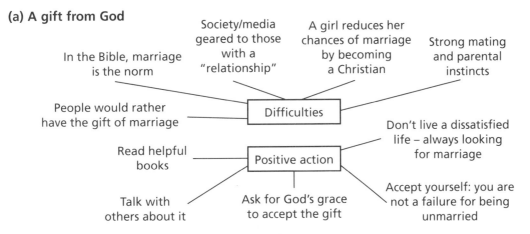

In the Bible, marriage is the norm

Society/media geared to those with a "relationship"

A girl reduces her chances of marriage by becoming a Christian

Strong mating and parental instincts

People would rather have the gift of marriage — Difficulties

Don't live a dissatisfied life – always looking for marriage

Read helpful books — Positive action

Talk with others about it

Ask for God's grace to accept the gift

Accept yourself: you are not a failure for being unmarried

(b) Can free us from earthly ties and worries

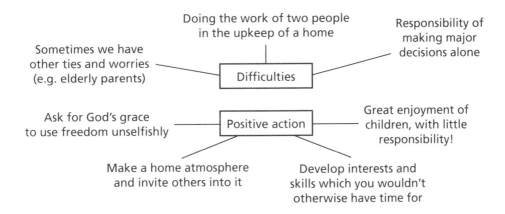

Doing the work of two people in the upkeep of a home

Responsibility of making major decisions alone

Sometimes we have other ties and worries (e.g. elderly parents) — Difficulties

Ask for God's grace to use freedom unselfishly — Positive action

Great enjoyment of children, with little responsibility!

Make a home atmosphere and invite others into it

Develop interests and skills which you wouldn't otherwise have time for

(c) Opportunity to give undivided attention to Jesus

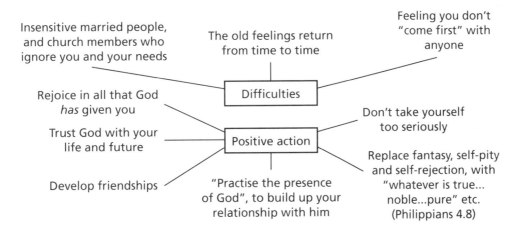

Insensitive married people, and church members who ignore you and your needs

The old feelings return from time to time

Feeling you don't "come first" with anyone

Difficulties

Rejoice in all that God *has* given you

Trust God with your life and future — Positive action

Develop friendships

"Practise the presence of God", to build up your relationship with him

Don't take yourself too seriously

Replace fantasy, self-pity and self-rejection, with "whatever is true... noble...pure" etc. (Philippians 4.8)

SESSION 6
Marriage and singleness

BLOCK 2: THIS YEAR, NEXT YEAR . . .

■ "Family" role plays

What the teenagers say to their parents or youth leaders

(a) "The minister said we shouldn't go out with someone if we're not seriously thinking of marrying them. You don't believe that, do you?"

(b) "How do you know when someone is the right person to marry?"

(c) "It's all right for you; you're married. But I might get left high and dry on the shelf. I don't see how anyone can stay sane on their own for the rest of their life."

(d) "My friend's parents are always having rows. I think they'd do better to get a divorce."

(e) "How far should my boy/girlfriend and I go physically?"

(f) "I don't see what would be wrong with living with my boy/girlfriend. We're in love, but we're not ready to tie ourselves down and get married. This could help us find out if we're suited to each other."

(g) "I have tried to get interested in boys/girls, but deep down I think I must be gay."

(h) "How do I clean out my mind from these impure thoughts which keep filling it?"

(i) "I feel so guilty because I keep giving way to masturbation, however hard I try not to."

Guide-passages and suggestions for "parents" or "youth leaders"

Do not rely on these suggestions if you can think of better arguments and passages to use.

(A) THE INTENTIONS BEHIND A RELATIONSHIP

If you understand the high value the Bible puts on singleness, and what a responsible task it is to discover God's choice of marriage-partner if he wants to give one, your answer will not be an easy "yes" or "no". The Bible contains no casual boyfriend – girlfriend relationships, but that is because they did not exist at that time.

1 Timothy 5.1–2 suggests the basic attitude to fellow-Christians which should guide us:

Do not rebuke an older man, but appeal to him as if he were your father. *Treat the younger men as your brothers*, the older women as mothers, and the *younger women as sisters*, with all purity. [Our italics.]

This suggests that boy-girl friendships, which are certainly not forbidden, should be taking place openly within the Christian family, helpful to each other's faith, and seeking to give support rather than gain "street cred" with your friends. Two Christian friends should be honest with each other about how they see the future, and should be open to God making it clear to them at the right time if he wants them to get married.

(B) FINDING YOUR LIFE-PARTNER

The principles are largely the same as in any need for God's guidance. They are well expressed in Proverbs 3.5–6:

Trust in the LORD with all your heart. Never rely on what you think you know. Remember the LORD in everything you do, and he will show you the right way.

Paul gives more earthy, but very realistic, advice in 1 Corinthians 7.8–9.

Now, to the unmarried and to the widows I say that it would be better for you to continue to live alone as I do. But if you cannot restrain your desires, go ahead and marry — it is better to marry than to burn with passion.

When someone makes you *want* to marry them, *and* fulfils the qualifications you agreed in Block 1, it is a very positive sign!

(C) LIFE WITHOUT A PARTNER

Jesus spoke about this in Matthew 19.11–12, using the picture of being a eunuch, i.e. unable to produce children, which was central to the Jewish understanding of marriage. He includes those who are divorced, separated and widowed as well as the never (yet) married.

Not everyone can accept this teaching, but only those to whom it has been given. For some are eunuchs because they were born that way; others were made that way by men; and others have renounced marriage because of the kingdom of heaven. The one who can accept this should accept it. (NIV)

His crucial point is that he will give us only what we can cope with, and we should learn to accept what he gives us, not sour our lives by resenting it. If we fear loneliness, for example, we should make the most of a range of ordinary friends, instead of searching for one special friend to meet all our needs.

(D) DIVORCE

The law of the land allows divorce if there is "irretrievable breakdown" of marriage. And some would say that point had arrived if the couple are always arguing. But Jesus teaches that marriage is made of stronger stuff than that in Mark 10.2–9.

> Some Pharisees came to him and tried to trap him. "Tell us," they asked, "does our Law allow a man to divorce his wife?" Jesus answered with a question, "What law did Moses give you?" Their answer was, "Moses gave permission for a man to write a divorce notice and send his wife away." Jesus said to them, "Moses wrote this law for you because you are so hard to teach. But in the beginning, at the time of creation, 'God made them male and female,' as the scripture says. 'And for this reason a man will leave his father and mother and unite with his wife, and the two will become one.' So they are no longer two, but one. No human being then must separate what God has joined together."

God designed marriage to be permanent. Although the New Testament seems to accept divorce as a sad possibility in two cases – one partner being unfaithful (Matthew 19.9) or refusing to go on living with a newly converted Christian (1 Corinthians 7.15) – God would always much rather help the couple to repair their marriage.

(E) HOW FAR TO GO?

The one clear guideline in the Bible is that sexual intercourse belongs to marriage alone (Genesis 2.24); united bodies should wait for united lives. Beyond this, the Bible gives no chart of when it is right to hold hands, kiss, etc.! It is a matter for the two friends to decide maturely and prayerfully together.

(F) LIVING TOGETHER

The remarkable sentence Genesis 2.24 gives God the Creator's instructions about living together.

> That is why a man leaves his father and mother and is united with his wife, and they become one.

Both Jesus and Paul quote it as "the last word" (as well as the first!) on the subject. Only the lifelong commitment of marriage gives the security for two human beings to live together in full unity. Sadly, 75 per cent of unmarried cohabiting couples break up. Obviously some of them want to retain the freedom to move on; but others are hoping for a permanent relationship, and would stand a better chance of finding it by waiting (if need be) for the right moment to get married. This does not mean that we should condemn couples who are already living together; we should encourage them to move on to the greater commitment and unity of marriage.

(G) HOMOSEXUALITY

There is no excuse for the abuse which Christians have heaped on gay people through history. Parents may naturally be shocked at discovering that one of their children is gay, but the real Christian response is to show concern, tenderness and acceptance. The Bible outlaws homosexual intercourse in several places, for example, 1 Corinthians 6.9–10:

> Surely you know that the wicked will not possess God's Kingdom. Do not fool yourselves; people who are immoral or who worship idols or are adulterers or homosexual perverts or who steal or are greedy or are drunkards or who slander others or are thieves – none of these will possess God's Kingdom.

But it seems never to speak directly about being attracted to people of your own sex, which often the person experiencing it cannot help. He or she should realize that many people go through a "same-sex feelings" phase in their teens, from which they gradually emerge. They should not too quickly label themselves gay.

(H) IMPURE THOUGHTS

We win the battle by feeding our minds a pure diet. We cannot help the first thought; but we can discourage it from lingering and leading to action. 2 Samuel 11.2 reads:

> One day, late in the afternoon, David got up from his nap and went to the palace roof. As he walked about up there he saw a woman having a bath. She was very beautiful.

David's temptation is common to very many human beings. But giving in to it eventually led him to commit murder and adultery. It is important to learn to draw on God's help to keep our minds in tune with what he wants.

(I) MASTURBATION

The Bible never mentions masturbation, which should stop us forming hard and fast rules, which may impose purely human guilt on people. Some people find masturbation impossible to separate from lustful fantasies; in which case Jesus' words in Matthew 5.27–28 may well apply to them:

> You have heard that it was said, "Do not commit adultery". But now I tell you: anyone who looks at a woman and wants to possess her is guilty of committing adultery with her in his heart.

They should pray for God's forgiveness, and for his strength to say no to what is wrong. But some find no automatic connection with fantasies, and have experienced real liberation from depressing guilt feelings by seeing masturbation as God's provision for their sexual needs.

■ Session 7 ■

The Holy Spirit

AIM

The fellowship and encouragement of the Holy Spirit make a resoundingly positive note on which to end Series 1. In addition, the gifts he has given to each member of Christ's Body, in order to serve others, point to the main purpose of this course: finding and learning how to carry out the job God wants me to do in my church.

The material in this session tries hard to be unbiased and uncontroversial! We have deliberately left out any reference to the baptism or fullness of the Holy Spirit, because different churches teach different things. We encourage you to add a section of your own if you want to. But your course may contain people from different churches or with different emphases about spiritual gifts and the Holy Spirit. If so, it may be worth reminding them at the beginning to respect and be sensitive to each other. The point of the session is to help each other grow more confident and useful in serving Jesus. So it may be better to concentrate on what we can all agree on than to end up arguing.

BLOCK 1: THE GIFT OF THE SPIRIT

1. What does the Spirit mean to you?

Sharing   15 mins

In pairs of people who know each other well ask them to share what they see as some of the ways in which God's Holy Spirit has been changing their lives in recent months. If your course have not done home assignments, they will probably appreciate 5 minutes of silence; perhaps with paper and pen to reflect on the question, before answering it. If they have done either of the home assignments in the members' pages, they may refer to what they wrote.

2. Who exactly is the Holy Spirit and what is the purpose of the Holy Spirit?

Bible study   20 mins

Join the pairs up into groups of four and distribute members' pages 72–74. They should work together on both questions under "Who exactly is the Holy

Spirit?". After 8 or 9 minutes, move them on to "What is the purpose of the Holy Spirit?" (section a) for another 5 or 6 minutes.

For the last 5 minutes, they should work on section (b) "Holy Spirit" on their own. Perhaps play some peaceful recorded music in the background during this. If they finish with time to spare, suggest they pray quietly. It may be appropriate for you to close this activity with a spoken prayer.

3. "Keep in step with the Spirit"

Trust exercise   10 mins

"Since we live by the Spirit, let us keep in step with the Spirit" is Paul's statement in Galatians 5.25 (NIV). To demonstrate it, ask for a volunteer to leave the room and be blindfolded. Get everyone else to form a human obstacle course round the floor of the room.

Appoint one person to be the voice of the Holy Spirit, guiding the blindfold "pilgrim" correctly to avoid the obstacles. Appoint someone else to be the voice of human nature, trying to drown the Spirit's voice with repeated contrary instructions; so leading the pilgrim into the obstacles. No-one else should speak.

Bring the pilgrim in, and explain to her or him what is going on, but not who the voices are; the pilgrim needs to learn which is the right voice, then listen to it, and follow it round the course. If there is time, let someone else have a go, and appoint two other voices. You could make it harder by having *three* "enemy" voices, representing world, flesh and devil!

At the end, ask the observers to comment on any ways they felt that the pilgrim's experience was like or unlike daily Christian living. Also comment on anything else they have learnt from the session so far; in particular, what has been helpful for throwing light on the common questions or misunderstandings of new Christians or those who have not yet started.

BLOCK 2: GIFTS OF THE SPIRIT

1. A complete list?

Bible study 10 mins

Ask everyone to get back together in the same groups of four as in Block 1, and distribute copies of the lists on pages 75–76 from the members' pages. Each person in the group should take one of the passages in section (a). In 4 to 5 minutes, they should list the gifts mentioned and then compare notes.

Then ask everyone to go on to section (b) for another 4 to 5 minutes. The groups should work together on compiling their extra list.

2. What gift or gifts has the Holy Spirit given you?

Self- and group-assessment 25 mins

Spend 5 minutes on section (c), asking people to work on their own. It may be a help if you introduce it by telling people what you have ticked as the gift or gifts you think you have.

Then ask them to spend 10 minutes doing the same exercise for the other members of the group (section (d)). Remind them that 1 Corinthians 12.7 says that every Christian reveals the Holy Spirit in some way; so they must find at least one gift in each group member. This assumes that the group members know each other reasonably well. You may need to rearrange groups slightly at the beginning of Block 2 to ensure this.

The climax of the block is section (e) (also 10 minutes), where people have the chance to point out the gifts they see in each other. If handled gently and positively, this can be enormously reassuring to people and can build up their confidence. Be aware that your course will probably include some people who think they have no gifts at all, and possibly one or two who have inflated ideas of their own abilities. Prepare them light-heartedly for the shock this exercise will bring them: "If you think you have *no* spiritual gifts, you're in for a pleasant surprise. The Holy Spirit gives at least one gift to *every* Christian; and if you can't see what yours is, almost certainly your friends can. If, on the other hand, you think you've got every gift in the list, this could be a rude awakening for you; the Holy Spirit does not give all the gifts to one person, and your friends are the best people to know which ones you haven't got!"

3. Reflection

 10 mins

Let people meditate on section (f) on their own. Again, it might be good to play some background music, and to round things off with a closing prayer.

Tell people that you are available if they want to talk about any thoughts they have had during section (f); or they may prefer to talk to others on the course. Be ready to advise people on any developments they may want to suggest in the part they play in church life. Remind them there will be further time to reflect and learn during the rest of *Ready to Serve*.

SESSION 7
The Holy Spirit

BLOCK 1: THE GIFT OF THE SPIRIT

■ Who exactly is the Holy Spirit?

Look up John 14.15–18, and discuss it with your group. Note the following facts that Jesus gives about the Holy Spirit; for each one, fill in the verse from which it is drawn, and complete any blanks.

(a) In many ways he is just the same as Jesus:

- like Jesus, he is *another* .... (verse ....)
- like Jesus, he teaches the truth about God (verse ....)
- like Jesus, he is not understood by the .... around (verse ....)
- he is so like Jesus, that Jesus describes his coming as: "I will ...." (verse ....)

(b) But in some ways he is different from Jesus' life on earth:

- Jesus was with his disciples for only three years; but the Holy Spirit will be with them (and us) for .... (verse ....)
- Jesus was visible as a human being; but the Holy Spirit cannot be .... (verse ....)
- Jesus was a separate person *alongside* his friends; but the Holy Spirit will actually live .... them (verse ....)

From this passage, it is possible to identify the Holy Spirit as Jesus' other self living inside his followers.

■ And what is the purpose of the Holy Spirit?

Jesus in John 14 calls the Holy Spirit a "Helper" or "Counsellor" (NIV) who is with us as God's presence. Here are two other names that the New Testament gives to the Holy Spirit. They point to two of the most important jobs he does on earth. Continue in small groups to work through question (a).

For **Ready to Serve** course use only © Bible Society 1995

(a) "Life-giving Spirit"

Look up Romans 8.1–2.

(i)   In the left-hand column are four phrases from this passage, spelling out the change that the Holy Spirit makes in those who become Christians. In the right-hand column, in a different order, are explanations of each phrase. Fill in the numbers in the brackets, so that each explanation on the right matches its corresponding phrase on the left.

(1) No condemnation	( ) Christians share the whole of their lives with Jesus; and he shares his with them.
(2) those who live in union with Christ	( ) The Holy Spirit brings life wherever he goes, so he "automatically" makes people spiritually alive when he enters their experience.
(3) the law of the Spirit, which brings us life	( ) He reverses the equally automatic system under which sinfulness cut us off from God.
(4) set me free from the law of sin and death	( ) This is because he makes real the forgiveness Jesus achieved by dying for us.

(ii) When do you think the Spirit brought you to life?

(b) "Holy Spirit"

(Study this section on your own.)
Look up Galatians 5.16–17.

(i)   Think of an example from your own experience of the kind of struggle mentioned in verse 17. Who won?

....

....

(ii) Look on to verses 19–21. Look back over the list and confess to God any areas where your human nature is still holding out against the Holy Spirit. This cat-alogue of human nature is here broken down into sub-sections. Under each sub-section write down an example of this type of behaviour today.

immoral, filthy, indecent actions

....

worship of idols and witchcraft

....

people become enemies and they fight

....

they become jealous, angry and ambitious

....

they separate into parties and groups

....

they get drunk, have orgies, etc.

....

(iii) Look on to verses 22–23. Tick any areas where you feel the Holy Spirit has made any improvement in you over the last year:

☐ LOVE　　☐ JOY　　☐ PEACE　　☐ PATIENCE　　☐ KINDNESS
☐ GOODNESS　☐ FAITHFULNESS　☐ HUMILITY　　☐ SELF-CONTROL

This list is the best test there is of how far God's Holy Spirit has taken your life in hand.
How are you getting on?

SESSION 7

The Holy Spirit

BLOCK 2: GIFTS OF THE SPIRIT

■ A complete list?

(a) Give each member of the group one of these passages to look up, and list the spiritual gifts mentioned. For the moment ignore the boxes on the right.

1 Corinthians 12.8–10　　　　　You　　　　The others

	You	The others		
(1)	[ ]	[ ]	[ ]	[ ]
(2)	[ ]	[ ]	[ ]	[ ]
(3)	[ ]	[ ]	[ ]	[ ]
(4)	[ ]	[ ]	[ ]	[ ]
(5)	[ ]	[ ]	[ ]	[ ]
(6)	[ ]	[ ]	[ ]	[ ]
(7)	[ ]	[ ]	[ ]	[ ]
(8)	[ ]	[ ]	[ ]	[ ]
(9)	[ ]	[ ]	[ ]	[ ]

1 Corinthians 12.28

(1)	[ ]	[ ]	[ ]	[ ]
(2)	[ ]	[ ]	[ ]	[ ]
(3)	[ ]	[ ]	[ ]	[ ]
(4)	[ ]	[ ]	[ ]	[ ]
(5)	[ ]	[ ]	[ ]	[ ]
(6)	[ ]	[ ]	[ ]	[ ]
(7)	[ ]	[ ]	[ ]	[ ]
(8)	[ ]	[ ]	[ ]	[ ]

Romans 12.6–8

(1)	[ ]	[ ]	[ ]	[ ]
(2)	[ ]	[ ]	[ ]	[ ]
(3)	[ ]	[ ]	[ ]	[ ]
(4)	[ ]	[ ]	[ ]	[ ]
(5)	[ ]	[ ]	[ ]	[ ]

(6) ....   [ ]   [ ]   [ ]   [ ]

(7) ....   [ ]   [ ]   [ ]   [ ]

Ephesians 4.11

(1) ....   [ ]   [ ]   [ ]   [ ]

(2) ....   [ ]   [ ]   [ ]   [ ]

(3) ....   [ ]   [ ]   [ ]   [ ]

(4) ....   [ ]   [ ]   [ ]   [ ]

NB the last two words probably constitute *one* gift.

(b) Cross out the second (or more) mention of any one gift in (a). You now
have a full list of most of the spiritual gifts named in the New Testament.
There is no hint that it is a closed list. Think of at least five other gifts or
abilities you have seen in use in your church or another one:

(1) ....   [ ]   [ ]   [ ]   [ ]

(2) ....   [ ]   [ ]   [ ]   [ ]

(3) ....   [ ]   [ ]   [ ]   [ ]

(4) ....   [ ]   [ ]   [ ]   [ ]

(5) ....   [ ]   [ ]   [ ]   [ ]

....   [ ]   [ ]   [ ]   [ ]

....   [ ]   [ ]   [ ]   [ ]

....   [ ]   [ ]   [ ]   [ ]

■ Which gift or gifts has the Holy Spirit given you?

(c) Now on your own, work through the list above, ticking in the first column
any of these gifts that you think you may possess. If you believe you have a
gift in Christ's service different from anything in the list, add it below. Do
this carefully and prayerfully, remembering what the Holy Spirit gives
spiritual gifts for:

"The Spirit's presence is shown in some way in each person for the good of
all" (1 Corinthians 12.7).

(d) Go through the list again and, in the next three columns, tick what you see
as the gift or gifts of the other members of your group. Again, add more
items to the list if you think that their gift is not on it.

(e) In your group, take it in turns to be quiet and let the others say what they see
as your spiritual gift or gifts; then tell them what you have listed for yourself.
This comparison can be a very good exercise in checking self-awareness, and

in learning how you appear to other people. If you find it hard to know what to say after people have pointed out what they see as your spiritual gift or gifts, just say thank you!

■ Reflection

(f) Finally, take time to think and pray over these questions on your own:
   (i) What have you learnt during this session?

   (ii) Is your church having the chance to use your spiritual gift or gifts?

   (iii) What do you think the Holy Spirit is asking you to do as a result of this session and series?

   How may he want to use or strengthen the way you help friends who are newer Christians than you, or who have not yet started as Christians?

Something to do at home

We strongly recommend that you do some further work at home between sessions of this series. This will help you go on thinking about the course, and begin to put what you are learning into practice.

■ (A) Basic level

These assignments help you to understand and apply one or two verses of Bible teaching on the topic you will be exploring at the next session. The assignments for sessions 3, 4 and 7 are adapted from John Chapman's Bible study sheets accompanying the course *Nurture in small groups*; this was part of the follow-up to the Billy Graham Crusade in Sydney, New South Wales.

Before session No. 2

WHY JESUS DIED

LOOK UP:	Mark 10.45
THINK:	Are there any words you don't understand?
	Find out what they mean, by asking someone else or looking in a dictionary.
NOTE:	"Son of Man" was Jesus' way of referring to himself.
READ:	Mark 10.32–45 to place Jesus' saying in its setting.

IN YOUR OWN WORDS: Rewrite Mark 10.45 to make its meaning clear:

....

....

....

....

(a) Jesus says: he did* / did not* come to be served.

(* cross out the wrong word(s))

But does he deserve to be served as someone in authority?

Yes*/No*

If so, why? ....

Who does he deserve to be served by?

....

....

THINK IT OVER: In what ways do you serve Jesus as your King?

....

....

(b) Jesus says he came to give his life on the cross to set people free (part of the meaning of "redeem" or "ransom").
From verse 34, list what the Gentiles (Romans) did to him after the Jews condemned him to death:

(1) ....   (2) ....

(3) ....   (4) ....

THINK IT OVER: Jesus went through this for you.

- Have you ever thanked him?
- Why not do so (again) now?

(c) Jesus says his death on the cross was an example of serving other people.
- Why did you need Jesus to serve you by dying for you?

....

....

(If you are not sure of the answer to this question, ask your course-leader at the next session.)

In verses 43 and 44, Jesus says that the person who wants to share his greatness must:

(1) ....

(2) ....

THINK IT OVER: In what ways do you (or should you) serve other people, especially other Christians?

....

....

LEARN BY HEART: Mark 10.45. (It will help you to love and follow Jesus.)

Before session no. 3

THE BIBLE

LOOK UP: 2 Timothy 3.16–17
THINK: Are there any words you don't understand?
READ: 2 Timothy 3.10–17 to place the verses in their setting.

IN YOUR OWN WORDS: Rewrite 2 Timothy 3.16–17 to make its meaning clear:

....

....

....

....

....

(a) Which part of the Bible is "inspired" or "breathed" by God?

....

As the Greek word which we translate "inspired" means "breathed out", who is the final author of the Bible?

....

THINK IT OVER: What should your attitude to the Bible be?

....

(b) From this passage, what four things is the Bible useful for?

(1) .... (2) ....

(3) .... (4) ....

THINK IT OVER: Are you missing out on any of these uses of the Bible?

(c) What sort of person will the Bible be useful to? ....
What will the Bible do for this person?

....

Beyond the Bible, what more will this person need to know?

....

THINK IT OVER: What do you need to do to make verse 17 more true of you?

....

What would be a good routine of Bible study for you to adopt?

....

....

LEARN: 2 Timothy 3.16–17

Before session No. 4

CHURCH

LOOK UP: Hebrews 10.24–25

THINK: Are there any words you don't understand?

READ: Hebrews 10.19–25 to place the verses in their
                 setting.

IN YOUR OWN WORDS: Rewrite Hebrews 10.24–25 to spell out its meaning:

....

....

....

....

....

(a) What two things should we help our fellow-Christians to do, according to verse 24?

(1) ....   and (2) ....

THINK IT OVER: How might you help your fellow-Christians to do these things?

....

....

....

(b) What should we not give up doing? ....

THINK IT OVER: Why do some Christians give this up?

....

....

Why should we not give it up?

....

....

(c) What is one of the main purposes of church meetings, according to verse 25?

....

And why, does it say, should we do this "all the more"?

....

THINK IT OVER: What is this "Day"? ....

What difference does its approach make to you and your church?

....

Who in your church encourages you to show love and to do good?

....

Who are you encouraging to show love and to do good?

....

LEARN: Hebrews 10.24–25

Before session No. 5

DOUBTS

LOOK UP: Hebrews 11.1
THINK: Are there any words you don't understand?
READ: Hebrews 10.32—11.3 to place this verse in its setting.

IN YOUR OWN WORDS: Rewrite Hebrews 11.1 to make clear what you think the writer meant by it:

....

....

....

(a) In what two ways does Hebrews 11.1 describe faith?

   (1) ....

and (2) ....

THINK IT OVER: What are some of your hopes as a Christian?

....

....

....

What are some of the realities you believe in as a Christian, which you cannot see?

....

....

....

For **Ready to Serve** course use only © Bible Society 1995

How sure and certain are you about them?

(b) What truth about God do we understand by faith, according to Hebrews 11.3?

....

....

THINK IT OVER: Do you have doubts about what God has done in the past?

....

....

Do you have doubts about what God can do? ....

....

What is the cure for them? ....

....

(c) List four ways that the Hebrew Christians had suffered, according to Hebrews 10.33–34.

(1) ....

(2) ....

(3) ....

(4) ....

In what truth did they have faith, which helped them to endure the suffering, according to verse 34?

....

What do you think the writer means by this?

....

THINK IT OVER: In what ways have you suffered as a Christian?

....

....

....

Has this caused you to doubt God's goodness or control?

....

....

In what precise way or ways does Hebrews 10.36 apply to you?

....

....

....

LEARN: Hebrews 11.1

Before session No. 6

MARRIAGE AND SINGLENESS

LOOK UP: Genesis 1.27

THINK: Are there any words you don't understand?

READ: Genesis 1.26–31 to place this verse in its setting.

IN YOUR OWN WORDS: Rewrite Genesis 1.27 to make clear what you think the author meant:

....

....

....

(a) What do you deduce from the setting to help you understand what God means by human beings being "like" him and "in his image"?

....

....

THINK IT OVER: How much do you consciously try to develop this image and likeness?

(b) In what sense do you think of "male and female" as showing us "God's likeness"?

....

....

THINK IT OVER: Do you think of God as the creator of your sexual feelings and attractions? Why not thank him for them now, and ask his help in directing them?

(c) THINK: How far does the fact that you are male or female influence:
- your major occupation
- your interests
- your opinions
- your ambitions

- your choice of friends
- your style of clothes
- your moods
- your personality?

LEARN: Genesis 1.27

Before session No. 7

THE HOLY SPIRIT

LOOK UP: Galatians 5.25

THINK: Are there any words you don't understand?

READ: Galatians 5.16–26 to place the verse in its setting.

IN YOUR OWN WORDS: Rewrite Galatians 5.25 to make clear what you think Paul meant by it:

....

....

....

(a) In verses 24 and 25, what two ways of living are contrasted?

(1) verse 24 ....

(2) verse 25 ....

What is the result of living the "natural" way, according to verse 21?

....

What have Christians done to their "sinful human" nature (verse 24)?

....

THINK IT OVER: Have you done away with your natural life and started afresh with the Holy Spirit? If so, how and when?

....

....

(b) What does it really mean to be controlled by (or keep in step with) the Spirit?

....

....

THINK IT OVER: How far is God's Spirit really in control of your life?

....

....

(c) What qualities of character should mark a Spirit-controlled life, according to verse 26?

....

....

What difficulties stand in the way of this, according to verse 17?

....

....

THINK IT OVER: What do you find difficult in living as a Christian?

....

....

How far are you overcoming those difficulties with the Holy Spirit's strength?

....

....

LEARN: Galatians 5.25

■ (B) Advanced level

In each assignment there is:

- **something to read** – read the Bible passages and ask, "What light does each throw on the subject of the next session?" If you are not sure what a passage means, ask for help from the leader or a fellow-member of your course.

- **something to write** – try to use the Bible passages to help you answer the written question.

Before session No. 2

WHY JESUS DIED

| Read: | John 10.1–18 | (Jesus' understanding of his death) |
| | Isaiah 53 | (The prophecy of the Suffering Servant dying for our sins) |

Ephesians 2.1–18 (Paul's view of what Jesus achieved)

Revelation 5   (John's vision of what Jesus achieved)

Write: Write an article called "What's so good about Good Friday?" for your church's outreach magazine , broadsheet, or Easter publicity. Try to include in your article what you have discovered from the Bible study. We suggest that the course-leader or members decide which is the best article and submit it for publication.

Before session No. 3

THE BIBLE

Read: 2 Timothy 3.14–17 (God's purpose in having the Bible written)

Luke 1.1–4   (An example of the human author's reliability)

Psalm 119.89–105 (Extract from a complete poem on the value of Bible in a believer's life)

1 Peter 1.10–12   (Old Testament prophecy in the light of the New

2 Peter 1.19–21   Testament)

Write: Imagine that a friend has written to you, saying that she or he is interested in becoming a Christian. The friend writes: "But I don't like the way you Christians keep going on about the Bible. What's so special about it?" Write your reply in letter form, and use the above passages to guide it.

Before session No. 4

CHURCH

Read: Acts 2.42–47   (The original church in action)

1 Corinthians 12.12–28 (An illustration of the church functioning healthily)

Hebrews 10.19–25   (The value of prayer and fellowship to a group of Christians under pressure to give up active church involvement)

1 Peter 2.4–12   (What you are committing yourself to as you become a member of Christ's Church)

Write: Write down, as a series of points, the things you would want to say to a young teenager who tells you, "I can be a good Christian without going to church". Suggest ways of getting involved in the church's life. Try to show the Bible's basis for what you say. You may know someone who thinks exactly that way; if so, go and tell that person your answer.

Before session No. 5

DOUBTS

Read: 1 John 1.1–2,6; 3.7–24; 5.1–14 (Extracts from a whole letter written to help us *know* that we have eternal life)

1 Corinthians 15.1–8 (The facts on which Christian faith is based)

Hebrews 10.32–11.3 (The challenge to hold on to our faith, even when it is tested)

Write: A list of any doubts that you have had at any time about the Christian faith. For those that you have been able to sort out, write down what you see as the answer to the doubt (and if possible, any part of the Bible that helped you find the answer).

If you have not had many doubts yourself, make a list of some common ones that you hear from other people, and how you would answer them from the Bible.

Before session No. 6

MARRIAGE AND SINGLENESS

Read: Genesis 1.26–31; 2.18–25 (God's original programme for human sexuality)

Matthew 1.18–25 (The decorum of Jesus' human parents)

1 Thessalonians 4.1–8 (Paul and his mission team's sex education lesson)

Write: Someone comes to you and says that they and their boy or girlfriend can see no reason why they should not sleep together, and then per-haps move in together. They're in love and are thinking seriously of getting married some time in the future, so why shouldn't they? They're both Christians. What would you say to them? (Try to go not only on what you think, but what the Bible says; by all means use other passages as well as those above.) Write down how you think (or hope!) the conversation would go between you and the person you are talking to.

Before session No. 7

THE HOLY SPIRIT

Read: Romans 8.1–17 (One of the most complete New Testament descriptions of life controlled by God's Spirit)

2 Corinthians 3 (The spiritual life, glory and freedom of the New Testament)

      Galatians 5.16–26   (The conflict between sin and holiness)

      Ephesians 3.14–21   (Prayer and praise for the Holy Spirit's activity)

Write: (For your benefit more than anyone else's) what you feel are some of the most important ways the Holy Spirit has been changing your life in recent months. Try to use the Bible passages as God's check-list to compare yourself with. If you prefer expressing this kind of thought in poetry, do so. Ask yourself as well: how would you expect a new Christian to begin becoming aware of the Holy Spirit in their life?

Making sense of the Bible

Introduction

Aim

This series of seven sessions builds up a method to enable us to make sense of any passage from the Bible that comes our way. In particular, it aims to improve the way we handle and explain the Bible in practical Christian service. It is the heart of the *Ready to Serve* course. We have placed it as the middle series or unit; but you could effectively start the course here. Psalm 119.125 makes a perfect motto-prayer: "I am your servant; give me understanding, so that I may know your teachings".

Content

The topics for the seven sessions are:
1. You can do it!
2. Why do people think the Bible's boring? (application)
3. Always look at the setting
4. The basic method
5. Words, words, words!
6. Inside information (historical background)
7. Picture language, poetry and parables

The sessions have been designed to run in this sequence. Most of them presuppose knowledge or skill acquired in previous sessions. It is not impossible to take the sessions in a different order, but you would need to adapt some of the activities in them.

Written exercises

Those from the members' pages form the staple diet of this series. They require honest, serious thought, and are quite demanding in places. This is the most stretching part of the course, because making sense of the Bible is hard work; but it is immensely rewarding, as it leads to greater effectiveness in our ministry to other Christians and to friends interested in Christianity. The leader may need to give some course members a great deal of help and encouragement.

"Something to do at home"

If you plan to set course members home assignments at Basic Level (pages 153–155), you need to choose which of the several options to set for each session. The final one each time refers to the "set book". This would be one book of the Bible, which you choose, for everyone to study alongside this series. It could, for instance, be a book currently being studied in any Bible-reading notes your course members use; or it could form the basis of your church's Sunday teaching programme. Each time you will need to select suitable passages from it for the assignment. The Advanced Level assignments take Matthew's Gospel in exactly this way (pages 155–156).

■ Session 1 ■

You can do it!

A I M

Making sense of the Bible is at the heart of all effective Christian ministry. So we aim in this first session to reassure people that they really can learn to understand what the Bible says and explain it to someone else. We do this both from what the Bible teaches and by a short practice.

BLOCK 1: YOU REALLY CAN!

LEADER'S NOTES

1. Guess who

Party game   5 mins

It is important, if this series is to succeed, that those taking part get on well together. So it is always good to begin with a few minutes' fun and relaxation, sometimes even a party game.

In addition, it is important at this stage to boost people's confidence in handling the Bible. Many people take fright at the idea of being able to understand it for themselves.

If your course has more than eight members, split them into two or more groups of at least four people, at most eight. A volunteer from each group comes to you in the middle; you tell them the name of a Bible character; they go back to the group to mime the character; the others guess who it is, and the only words the volunteer may say are "yes" and "no". When somebody guesses correctly they come to you with the answer, and you tell them the next name.

If you think it would be too threatening to mime alone (or there are people with very little Bible knowledge), they could work in twos or threes.

Suggested list of Bible characters:

Samson (and Delilah)	Paul
Peter	Daniel
Eve (and Adam)	John the Baptist
Pontius Pilate	Jonah
David (and Goliath)	Mary Magdalene

Stop after 5 minutes; the team ahead at that point is the winner. Do not let this event drag on, or leave one group idle while others catch up. The important thing is to congratulate people on demonstrating such a wealth of Bible knowledge!

2. You can do it! You really can!

Discussion   20 mins

Give everyone a copy of members' page 97. Arrange people in pairs or threes. In each of the three questions people start on their own, then share their thoughts with their neighbours. Try to keep the private reflection to 3 minutes maximum each time, and the discussion to 3 minutes maximum.

(a) "An instant Bible survey" aims to start people talking about how they use the Bible. Those who are finding the Bible helpful should encourage any who have difficulties with it.

(b) "Bible unbook!" aims to help people see something of the Bible's value by imagining what things would be like if it didn't exist.

(c) "Nobody agrees what it means" unearths some common opinions of interpretation, the real subject of this series. At the end of this part, take a quick show of hands on how many SAs, As, etc., for each opinion. Tell everyone that this series aims to make understanding the Bible easier.

3. Who does the Bible expect to be able to make sense of it?

Bible research   20 mins

Assign one of the passages on page 98 to each course member. They should look it up, work out how it answers the question and report back after 5 minutes to the rest of the course.

If your numbers are large, and you have more than one person looking at each passage, ask *one* to report back, and the other(s) only to comment if they have anything different to add.

As a rough guide, our understanding of the general drift of these passages is:

(a) The Bible is basically clear, and is rightly understood by those who try to obey it (Psalm 119.99–100) and serve God (Psalm 119.125), regardless of their intellectual ability or training (Acts 4.8–13).

(b) Our understanding grows as we gradually and steadily mature as Christians (2 Timothy 3.14–15), without getting stuck at the elementary stage (Hebrews 5.11–14), or blown off course by distorted explanations (2 Peter 3.15–17).

(c) But because of the harder parts of the Bible (2 Peter 3.16), we need the help of dedicated, gifted Bible teachers (Nehemiah 8.7–8; 1 Timothy 4.13–14; 2 Timothy 3.16–17 where we understand "the person who serves God" to mean not "every Christian", but Bible teachers such as Timothy).

At the end, discuss as a full course whether you feel encouraged or discouraged by the exercise. If anyone is discouraged, tell them that Block 2 should redress the balance.

BLOCK 2: HOW TO SET ABOUT IT

This block aims to start people explaining simple parts of the Bible immediately.

1. Have a go!

Role play

20 mins

Hold a role play, ideally in pairs where partner A pretends to have just started as a Christian and knows nothing. Partner B explains the Lord's Prayer (Matthew 6.9–13) to her or him for 5 minutes. They then discuss for 5 minutes how partner B got on in making clear what this part of the Bible means. Perhaps ask for some Bs to tell the rest of the course something they found helpful in what their A said.

Then reverse the process with the "Grace" (2 Corinthians 13.13), A explaining to B. It is quite possible to take 5 minutes to explain the ideas in this to a brand-new Christian, but it would be better to tell people they have got 2 or 3 minutes and stop then, unless they are still in full flight. Use the next 5 or more minutes to check how people have got on, answer questions, etc. Encourage them that in explaining the Bible to someone else, they have done something vitally important.

If some members of your course really are new Christians, or are hesitant about role play, divide people into larger groups with an audience of observers watching two more experienced role players.

2. "He will not suffer thy foot to be moved"

Discussion

5 mins

Explain that it is possible to misunderstand some parts of the Bible. Tell the story of the Christian Army Officer wounded in battle, whose doctor had advised a foot amputation. The patient asked to have time to pray and as he flicked through his Authorised Version of the Bible, his eye fell on Psalm 121.3a, "He will not suffer thy foot to be moved". He took this as divine guidance that he should refuse the operation, and did so; his foot recovered! (GNB translates this line as "He will not let you fall".)

What do the course members think of this method of understanding the Bible – and why?

Our opinion is that it is a complete misuse of the Bible, breaking several of the "commandments" which follow, despite the positive outcome of the story. Fundamentally, as the modern translations show, it misunderstands what the older version meant by "be moved".

3. Ten commandments for making sense of the Bible

Input   20 mins

Ask everyone to look through the "Ten Commandments" from the members' pages 99–100 all together. Add any comments of your own; and encourage course members to chip in with any comments; such as a reason why a commandment is important or, if they are aware of any, examples of what goes wrong when someone disobeys one of the "commandments". Do not stifle any helpful comments, but keep this moving fairly briskly.

If there is time, move people on to the next activity in the members' pages; they should work on it in pairs or threes. The idea is simply to link one Bible passage to each commandment, but not everyone will find it easy: be available to help. For example some people may not know that "the Book of Moses" (Mark 12.26) refers to a book, or group of books, in the Bible.

We see the Bible passages matching the "commandments" as follows:

(1) 1 Corinthians 2.13–14
(2) Psalm 119.36,104
(3) Psalm 119.44
(4) Mark 12.19,26
(5) Matthew 4.5–7
(6) Mark 10.2–9
(7) Matthew 23.23
(8) Mark 2.23–27
(9) 1 Corinthians 13.9–10,12
(10) 2 Corinthians 4.2

But some of the passages could probably go with other commandments equally well. So do not let people sweat blood over this!

Explain that the important thing is that there are clear guidelines to help us make sense of the Bible. Several of these "commandments" will be the subject of whole sessions later in the series, e.g. commandment 3 in session 2, commandments 4 and 5 in session 3. Perhaps finish with a prayer based on commandment 1.

LEADER'S NOTES

You can do it!

BLOCK 1: YOU REALLY CAN!

■ You can do it! You really can!

(a) An instant Bible survey

(i) Fill in your answers to this short questionnaire (be honest!):

When did you last look at a Bible? ....

For what purpose? ....

Did you get what you wanted from it? ....

If not, why not? ....

(ii) Compare your answers with the one or two people sitting next to you.

(b) Bible unbook!

(i) Imagine that the Bible does not exist and never has.
What difference would this make to your life as a Christian? Think about it for 2 or 3 minutes!

(ii) Compare your thoughts with the same one or two people.

(c) Nobody agrees what it means

(i) Here are three opinions which many people hold:
- Trying to make sense of difficult parts of the Bible on my own would be beyond me.
- There are so many different "interpretations" (or ways of explaining the difficult parts) that it's impossible to know the right one.
- I'm going to steer clear of the difficult parts, and stick to what is easy and obvious.

Write beside each opinion what you think of it, using this code:

SA (= strongly agree), A (= agree), N (= not sure), D (= disagree),
SD (= strongly disagree).

(ii) Compare your opinion with the same one or two people.

■ Who does the Bible expect to be able to make sense of it?

How does each of these passages answer the question above?

Psalm 119.99–100 ....

....

Psalm 119.125 ....

....

Acts 4.8–13 ....

....

2 Timothy 3.14–17 ....

....

Hebrews 5.11–14 ....

....

2 Peter 3.15–17 ....

....

Nehemiah 8.7–8 ....

....

1 Timothy 4.13–14 ....

....

You can do it!

BLOCK 2: HOW TO SET ABOUT IT

■ Ten commandments for making sense of the Bible

(1) You shall pray for God the Holy Spirit's help in understanding the Bible, as he is the overall author.

(2) You shall allow what the Bible teaches to mould your opinions – and not vice versa!

(3) You shall constantly try to obey the Bible's teaching in daily life.

(4) You shall always look at the passage's setting.

(5) You shall check whether the real meaning of a passage is what it seems at first sight to say.

(6) You shall, where possible, use one part of the Bible to make sense of another.

(7) You shall not ignore the bits you don't like!

(8) You shall not over-emphasize one truth out of proportion, so that it contradicts something else the Bible teaches.

(9) You shall not be too sure this side of heaven that your understanding is always right!

(10) You shall never twist the Bible's words to win your point.

Each of the following passages gives the reason for one of the "Ten commandments for making sense of the Bible". With your working partner, try to work out which passage belongs best with which commandment.

You may think that some of the passages, especially the last few, cover more than one commandment. Don't worry – make the best arrangement you can in the time!

Passage	*Commandment*
Psalm 119.44	....
(A poem to God about his laws recorded in the Bible.)	
1 Corinthians 2.13–14	....
(NB Paul's "we" refers to the apostles – the original teachers and writers of the New Testament.)	
1 Corinthians 13.9–10,12	....
(Paul compares life on earth now with the better things to come in heaven.)	
2 Corinthians 4.2	....
(Paul and Timothy's policy of never altering what God has said.)	

Passage	Commandment
Psalm 119.36,104	....
(The Bible affects the psalm-writer's deepest thoughts.)	
Matthew 23.23	....
(Jesus condemns the Pharisees for obeying parts of the law, while forgetting about other parts.)	
Matthew 4.5–7	....
(The devil quotes the Bible – but does it really mean what he says?)	
Mark 12.18–27, especially 19,26	....
(Jesus answers the Sadducees from something else that Moses wrote.)	
Mark 2.23–27	....
(Jesus uses another part of the Bible to correct the Pharisees' wrong emphasis.)	
Mark 10.2–9	....
(The Pharisees have latched on to one part of the Bible, but Jesus uses another to show what it really means.)	

Remember – you *can* do it!

■ Session 2 ■

Why do people think the Bible's boring?

AIM

A golden key to making sense of the Bible is to remember what it is. Not just ancient history, but a book God means us to live by today. Our reason for understanding it should always be to respond positively to what God is saying to us through it. "Explain your law to me, and I will obey it; I will keep it with all my heart" (Psalm 119.34).

BLOCK 1: THE CHIEF REASON

1. Well, why?

Discussion   5 mins

Ask the full course (or smaller subgroups) why they think the Bible has such a bad image, and whether *they* have ever found the Bible boring; if so, why? Encourage them to be honest; confess to any times that you have found it less than riveting yourself. If you think your course members are far too good Christians to call the Bible boring, rephrase the question: "Are there times when you would rather watch something on TV than read the Bible?" Once they start giving honest answers, be unshockable!

2. How to avoid dynamic Bible reading

Drama and discussion   10 mins

Well ahead of this session, ask a good actor or confident character to be prepared to perform the sketch on page 103 at this stage. Check that your actor has all the props they need.

Introduce your actor as Shirley or Sidney Sievebrain. The rest should then comment on what was wrong with her or his approach. There should be plenty to put right! One answer you are hoping for at some stage is, "She or he didn't try to find out what God was saying through the Bible". If it does not come within 5 minutes suggest it yourself.

3. It's boring if you don't "apply" it

Study   30 mins

Explain that although this is not the only reason, the Bible often seems boring because we are not using it properly. Often we are not asking, and so not hearing, "What is God wanting *me* to learn or do?" The Bible can never be boring if we are letting God shape our lives through it.

Ask everyone to work through each section of pages 104–107 on their own before sharing answers with two or three neighbours. Check that people are not getting bogged down. Rough timings for each section:

(a)   5 minutes;
(b)   5 minutes;
(c)   5 minutes;
(d)   15 minutes;

Section (d) is the hardest, and unless your course members are very experienced, you will probably need to help. It may be best to work through all or part of this section orally as a full course, with you checking that everyone understands. Get as far as you can in the time. For what it is worth, our suggestions for the underlying facts about God and Jesus, if you reach them, are something like:

Mark 6.8–11 – Jesus wanted his first servants to travel light to show that they relied on the welcome of the people they visited to tell about him; but if these people rejected Jesus' message, his servants must warn them – in language they would understand – of the consequences.

Joshua 1.5 – God stays close to his servants and helps them.

Philippians 4.2 – God wants Christians to sort out their disagreements.

Matthew 11.20–24 – God will judge people according to how much they know about him.

BLOCK 2: APPLICATION ALWAYS AND TODAY

1. "The Bible punched me on the nose!"

Sharing   5 mins

This was the way one person described the experience of something in the Bible "lighting up" and speaking directly to their needs and questions. Share the detail of any similar experience you may have had; be honest about what it meant to you at the time, and how you feel about it now (if that is any different). Encourage course members to be equally detailed and honest in sharing similar experiences of their own, if they have had any. Sum up that we cannot always expect the words to step off the page at us; but we can expect God to have something important for us to learn or re-learn, every time we read the Bible.

2. How to stop the Bible seeming boring

Study   35 mins

Ask people to follow on pages 108–110 from the members' pages, as you work aloud through the input in (ai). Explain that this is building on the foundations you laid in Block 1. Then go on to the example (aii). Explain the use of a, b and c in the verse number, 2 Corinthians 9.7; they are a standard way of referring to the different parts or phrases of the verse. When you are happy that people seem to have understood the example, ask them to start on the practice verses that follow (aiii). These derive Always Applications (AA) and Today Applications (TA) from Facts about God and Jesus (F). People should work on their own before sharing with two or three neighbours.

Then do the same with section (b), which works back to the facts behind what are already applications in the Bible. Work through the input and

example. The F should almost always begin "God (or Jesus or the Holy Spirit) . . ."; and it should usually deduce something about what God wants or likes (or dislikes!). The Bible passage may not state directly what that is but it implies it, for instance, the general principle which lies behind Mark 10.21. Our suggestion is along the lines of "God knows how easily human beings worship money, and put their faith in it instead of him. He wants us to turn our back on anything that would stop us following Jesus." Then let people work alone on the practice verses before sharing.

Rough timing if people are picking up the ideas here quickly:

(a)   not more than 15 minutes;

(b)   20 minutes.

You will need to be available to help individuals and small groups as they work on the practice pieces; the basic idea will seem very new and difficult to some of them. Just get as far as you can take them in the time.

As people work on the applications, keep pushing them beyond general moral advice for all Christians ("we should love each other") to the painful truth for them personally ("*I* should be kinder to Kevin")!

3. Prayer

                                                        5 mins

Group members should share one application that God has brought home to them in the session with the two or three neighbours they have been working with. They should then pray for each other.

If it is appropriate, round the session off by pointing out that it may be hard work to find out what God is saying to us through the Bible; and it may be uncomfortable, as he tells us to change the way we live. But it will never be *boring*!

How to avoid dynamic Bible reading

Props you need:
- Table and chair
- Waste-paper basket with newspaper in it
- Transistor radio
- Bible
- Book of Bible-reading notes

Shirley (or Sidney) Sievebrain enters, carrying Bible and book of Bible-reading notes. Sievebrain sits at the table.

Sievebrain: Fine. I've nothing else to do, so I'll get down to that Bible study I've been promising myself.

(Turns radio on, fairly quietly; picks up book of Bible-reading notes, and looks at first page.)

Now, what's this? "Three tips for reading the Bible."

(Turns radio up louder.)

"(1) Remember you are in God's presence. 'Be still, and know that I am God' (Psalm 46.10)."

(Gets up and rummages in waste-paper basket, from which Sievebrain retrieves newspaper.)

I'll have a look at this in a minute.

(Looks at notes again.)

Now, then. "(2) Pray that God will say something helpful to you through today's passage. 'Speak, Lord, for your servant is listening.'"

(Looks at radio, does not turn it off, but says:)

Sshh!

(From notes again:)

"1 Samuel 3.9. (3) Meditate on today's passage, and what it means for you. 'Do not let this Book of the Law depart from your mouth; meditate on it day and night, so that you may be careful to do everything written in it. Then you will be prosperous and successful' (Joshua 1:8)". Great verse, that. Meditate on it day and night. Great stuff.

(Closes book of notes. Looks at watch.)

Ah well, time for the news on telly now.

(Turns radio off, picks up books and goes out.)

© Lance Pierson

SESSION 2

Why do people think the Bible's boring?

BLOCK 1: THE CHIEF REASON

■ It's boring if you don't "apply" it

Applying the Bible's message to ourselves is asking: *"What is God wanting me to learn or do about this*?" in order to obey it.

Remember "Commandment" 3:

You shall constantly try to obey the Bible's teaching in daily life.

(a) So tick which of the following questions are helpful for applying a passage.

☐	How do you pronounce this Jewish name?
☐	How does another Bible version put it?
☐	Can I think of an example of this point?
☐	How will this work out in practice?
☐	What does this long word mean?
☐	When might I find this a real help to me?
☐	Is this a promise, warning, command or example?
☐	Is it poetry, history or straight teaching?
☐	What do I need to (re)learn from it?

(b) Have a try at applying the Bible:

1 Thessalonians 5.15 contains three general instructions which apply to all Christians. Work out when and how you could obey them in the next 24 hours:

Do not pay back wrong for wrong ....

....

Do good to fellow-Christians ....

....

Do good to everyone! ....

....

(c) A man who was seeking God's guidance by opening the Bible at random, stuck a pin in: "Judas went away and hanged himself". Trying again he happened on: "Go and do likewise". Making a final stab, he landed in: "What you are about to do, do quickly"! He disobeyed!

Clearly his method of guidance was all wrong: the Bible is for intelligent reading; it is not a pin-cushion!

But what was wrong with his method of applying the Bible to himself? Was he right, for instance, to assume that all these verses were direct commands from God to him?

....

....

(d) Many of the promises, commands, warning and examples in the Bible were for one particular person at one particular time. God will not necessarily deal with us the same way. *But there is always an underlying fact about God's character or will* behind the particular example. *That* is what we should apply.

Sometimes it is made clear in the Bible passage. For example, Hebrews 13.4.

Command: "Marriage should be honoured by all, and husbands and wives must be faithful to each other."

Fact about God: "God will judge those who are immoral and those who commit adultery."

Now try it yourself with Hebrews 13.5:

Command: ....

                  ....

                  ....

                  ....

Fact about God: ....

                  ....

                  ....

                  ....

Sometimes the underlying fact about God is not spelt out in the passage. For example, Colossians 3.20–21.

In verse 20 the fact *is* spelt out:

Command: "Children, it is your Christian duty to obey your parents always . . ."

Fact about God: ". . . for that is what pleases God."

In verse 21 the fact is not spelt out:

Command: "Parents, do not irritate your children, or they will become discouraged."

But it is not hard to see the underlying fact about God: something like, "God does not want children to be bitter or discouraged".

The examples we have looked at so far are very straightforward. They are general commands to all Christians, and so it is quite clear that the same command applies to us. The fact about God helps us to understand why he gives the command, but it does not change the command in any way.

But now look at Jesus' instructions to the twelve apostles in Mark 6.8–11. Why would these commands be difficult to carry out as they stand today?

....

....

....

What important facts about Jesus' character and how we should serve him do you think he was trying to express through the instructions to the apostles?

....

....

....

Which of those facts are still important for us to express as we try to follow Jesus and pass on his message?

....

....

....

How might we, in the twentieth century, put those facts into action?

....

....

....

For **Ready to Serve** course use only © Bible Society 1995

We need to "get back to the fact" about Jesus to help us apply his words today.

Now try working this out with some other examples.

What do you see as the *Fact about God* behind each of these passages?

Joshua 1.5 – a promise

....

....

Philippians 4.2 – a command

....

....

Matthew 11.20–24 – a warning

....

....

SESSION 2

Why do people think the Bible's boring?

BLOCK 2: APPLICATION ALWAYS AND TODAY

■ How to stop the Bible seeming boring

(a) Not one application, but two!

(i) INPUT

Recap: behind every section of the Bible we read lies a fact of unchanging truth about what God is like or what he has done, or how he wants his people to live. We need to work out how that fact should affect the way we live; this is called applying it.

But we usually need to look for two applications (pause for groans!):

(a) general application "for always", throughout our lives;

(b) particular application or action for today or tomorrow – what God is saying to us for the next 24 hours.

Sometimes a Bible passage helps us by stating the fact about God directly. Our job is simply to work out how it applies to us, throughout our lives and in the next 24 hours.

(ii) EXAMPLE

2 Corinthians 9.7, " . . . God loves the one who gives gladly", is an unchanging *fact* about God.

● The *always application* might be something like, "Therefore I shouldn't complain about giving money to my church"; i.e., a general guideline along the track of 9.7a and b: "Each man should give, then, as he has decided, not with regret or out of a sense of duty . . ."

● But the *today application* will express the impact of the fact about God on the next 24 hours: for example, "Give a generous donation to the charity who sent an appeal letter this morning"; "Is there a practical way in which I can help Gloria, who is a bit hard up at the moment?"; "Don't begrudge the cost of a long-distance telephone call to Mum tonight; she's feeling lonely."

(iii) PRACTICE

What do you think God means *you* to learn or do in the light of the facts about him (or Jesus) in the verses below?

	Always or in general	Today or tomorrow
John 10.28	....	....
	....	....
Hebrews 10.31	....	....
	....	....
Romans 5.8	....	....
	....	....

(b) Get back to the fact!

(i) INPUT

Sometimes a Bible passage states only the always application (AA) or today application (TA) for the first hearers or readers. We should not try to apply these to ourselves, but the fact (F) which lies behind them.

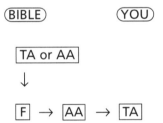

Always start on a Bible passage by asking:

(a) *Is this an F, an AA or a TA for the original hearers or readers?*
(b) *If an AA or a TA, what was the F at stake?*

(ii) EXAMPLE

Look up Mark 10.21 again.

● Some people think that Jesus wants *all* Christians to sell their belongings. But that is not necessarily so, because this is a TA for the man who came to see him. We need to get back to the fact about God which explains *why* he wanted this man to sell up.

● Jesus points toward the F in verses 23–25. He states the results for human beings of the fact about God. As always, we need to work out what this underlying fact about God's character and will is. Try putting it in your own words, beginning with "God . . ."

God ....

....

Whether or not the passage states the F, you should work out what it is, and then apply the F to you now. In this case, what would be your TA based on the F? (Perhaps the same as for the "rich young ruler"; perhaps very different)?

....

....

(iii) PRACTICE

Now try to work out what God is saying to *you* through each of these passages. Decide on the F (underlying fact about God or how he wants us to live); then *your* AA (always application) and TA (today application) in each case.

(a) Matthew 5.44–45

F God ....

AA ....

TA ....

(b) Psalm 116.1

F God ....

AA ....

TA ....

(c) Ephesians 4.29

F God ....

AA ....

TA ....

(d) Proverbs 15.1

F God ....

AA ....

TA ....

(e) Exodus 3.5

F God ....

AA ....

TA ....

■ **Session 3** ■

Always look at the setting

AIM

A second key to making sense of any passage in the Bible is to listen to it "in context", or in the setting in which it was written. This is one of the most important ways to understand what the original author meant.

BLOCK 1: THE IMMEDIATE SETTING

1. Blame it all on King James I!

Input

10 mins

Ask how many of the course are old enough to remember the King James translation or Authorized Version of the Bible. Do any of them still use it? Try shocking them by saying that some people think that the Authorized Version can actually hinder people from making sense of the Bible in English!

Go on to explain that the thought behind this has nothing to do with outdated language. Despite the many good features of this translation, it has the unhelpful practice of starting each verse on a new line. The original writers did not write their books in chapters and verses! Ever since the AV, Christians have suffered from the unfortunate tendency to look at each verse on its own, paying no attention to the surrounding words and sentences.

Demonstrate this by distributing copies of page 114 from the members' pages, which contrast the AV layout of 1 Corinthians 12.29—13.1 with an impression of how Paul's scribe would have written it down. The writing style of those days used capital letters only, no gaps between words and no punctuation! Readers were used to handling the lack of gaps and punctuation, and made sense of it all more easily than we might imagine.

But the most important difference was the lack of separate paragraphs. This means that we do not know for sure where the writer intended a change of subject. All later translators have imposed their own ideas about this. So we have also printed the paragraph without paragraph-breaks. From this we can see that "covet earnestly the best gifts" is not, as

it has so often been treated, a disembodied text, but refers back to the list in the previous verses; and the "more excellent way" is the "charity" or love of the next sentence.

2. Put each sentence in its immediate setting

Study

20 mins

Ask everyone to move on to the activity on page 115, which gives some practice at understanding the point you have been making. Work on section a all together. It seems clear to us that Paul is talking about Jesus' loving promise to stay with us through and beyond any form of persecution, however frightening. Check that people have understood.

Ask them to work on section (b) in their small groups of three or four. Check the kind of answers that people come up with. The point, as we understand it, is that Timothy is supposed to be helping the Christians in Ephesus stand firm against false teachers. Feeling young and insecure, he could be tempted to be argumentative, quarrelsome, impatient or aggressive. But, says Paul, that is not the mature Christian way to handle the challenge.

Ask people to work alone on section c and then compare notes with the others in their small group. (It seems quite wrong to apply Peter's words directly to schoolboys, because he is speaking to Christian wives!)

Rough timing for this 20-minute activity:

(a)   5 minutes;
(b)   10 minutes;
(c)   5 minutes.

LEADER'S NOTES

111

3. The setting can help you apply any Bible passage

Discussion and study   15 mins

Move people on to the study of Revelation 3.20 on page 118. In their groups of three or four they should look at the immediate setting to decide what the verse is really about.

You need to recognize that your course may contain people who came to faith through this verse. They may feel that this activity is questioning their experience. If you sense this reaction, you should reassure them that no-one is doubting their Christian commitment; merely whether Revelation 3.20 means exactly what they were told it meant at the time!

Take soundings after 7 or 8 minutes, and try to reach agreement on who the sentence is addressed to. Ask people to spend the last 4 or 5 minutes on their own, applying the verse to themselves. Obviously, the application will depend entirely on who you decide Jesus first addressed the verse to. If it is to Christians, then it is our lives he wants to enter; but is it our personal lives as separate people or our shared life together as a church? On the other hand, if you think Jesus was speaking to a lapsed church needing to start all over again, or to people who were never really Christians in the first place, our application may be to pass the message on in some way to people in that position.

BLOCK 2: THE WIDER SETTING OF THE SECTION, THE BOOK AND THE AUTHOR

1. The section

Study   15 mins

This is on page 117. Work on passage (a) "the lost son", all together. If you have people who are very new to the Bible and cannot do any of these exercises from memory, they can look up the passage immediately in order to check or test the others. When you have finished, explain that the beginning and end of the section or paragraph in which a passage comes, often helps us to understand it. Check that people have understood.

Ask people to work on passage (b) together in the small groups of three or four from Block 1.

2. The book

Study   10 mins

Explain that, nine times out of ten, the main thrust of the surrounding verses or section is the setting that really helps us to understand a passage. But sometimes it also helps us to know the wider setting of the book we are looking at. As we become familiar with the Bible, we begin to learn the main purpose of the different books.

Page 118 gives an example. Work on passage (a) together as a full course. Then ask people to work on (b) alone. As it is a confidential exercise, assure them that they will not have to show what they

write to anyone else. The key point, of course, is that John wrote his Gospel primarily to inspire faith in *enquirers*; and his letter to strengthen the faith of *Christians*.

3. The author

Study   20 mins

It sometimes helps, too, to know the setting of the book's author. As we work at making sense of the Bible we begin to get to know the way the different writers' minds work. Item (a) on pages 118–119 gives a simple example. Let people work in small groups or alone for 2 or 3 minutes.

Answers: (i) David the musician (Psalm 101.1);
(ii) Jesus the carpenter (Matthew 7.3, NIV);
(iii) Paul the tentmaker (with Timothy – 2 Corinthians 5.1);
(iv) Solomon the wise (Ecclesiastes 1.12–13, NIV);
(v) Luke the doctor (Luke 13.12–13).

Item (b) is a harder, but much more important, exercise. Allocate one author and passage to each individual.

(i) Paul, Romans 4.13–25;
(ii) James 2.14–26;
(iii) Writer to the Hebrews, 10.35—11.2.

Give them 5 to 6 minutes to work alone (or with a colleague, if they prefer) on the task of understanding what each writer appears to mean by "faith".

Spend the last 10 minutes or so hearing some answers and putting a final result on a board or OHP. Encourage people to write down your agreed answers. One possible set of definitions might be:

Paul – personal trust or commitment;
James – mental assent (what you believe in);
Hebrews – unshakeable confidence in unseen
resources and future rewards.

Point out that (i) this helps to make sense of individual sentences or passages in other parts of these authors' books (ii) they do not contradict each other, but put together several strands of what the Bible as a whole says about "faith".

Advance warning

Session 4, Block 1 needs course members to be able to study a reproduction of Holman Hunt's painting, *The Light of the World*. If you have not got access to a suitable copy, you can obtain either:

a poster print (approx 10" x 20") from Medici Society, 7 Grafton Street, London Wl 3LA (0171-629 5675) or through art shops

or post cards, from Medici Society, or from The Cathedral Bookshop, St Paul's Churchyard, London EC4M 8AD, often available through Christian bookshops;

The St Paul's Bookshop (0171-248 2705) also sell a slide of the painting in their slide-set 20B.

LEADER'S NOTES

SESSION 3

Always look at the setting

BLOCK 1: THE IMMEDIATE SETTING

■ Blame it all on King James I!

Some people have suggested that the Authorised Version (AV) can actually hinder people from making sense of the Bible in English!

Not because of the language, but because it printed each verse as a separate paragraph. Here is an example from 1 Corinthians 12.

AV as printed:

29. Are all apostles? Are all prophets? Are all teachers? Are all workers of miracles?

30. Have all the gifts of healing? Do all speak in tongues? Do all interpret?

31. But covet earnestly the best gifts: and yet shew I unto you a more excellent way.

CHAPTER 13
THOUGH I speak with the tongues of men and of angels, and have not charity, I am become as sounding brass or a tinkling cymbal.

AV without verse – paragraphs:

Are all apostles? Are all prophets? Are all teachers? Are all workers of miracles? Have all the gifts of healing? Do all speak in tongues? Do all interpret? But covet earnestly the best gifts: and yet shew I unto you a more excellent way. Though I speak with the tongues of men and of angels, and have not charity, I am become as sounding brass or a tinkling cymbal.

Effective impression of the original documents of same passage:

AREALLAPOSTLESAREALLPROPHETSAREALLTEACHERS
AREALLWORKERSOFMIRACLESHAVEALLTHEGIFTSOFHE
ALINGDOALLSPEAKINTONGUESDOALLINTERPRETBUTC
OVETEARNESTLYTHEBESTGIFTSANDYETISHEWUNTOYO
UAMOREEXCELLENTWAYTHOUGHISPEAKWITHTHETONGU
ESOFMENANDOFANGELSANDHAVENOTCHARITYIAMBECO
MEASSOUNDINGBRASSORATINKLINGCYMBALANDTHOUG

For **Ready to Serve** course use only © Bible Society 1995

Remember "Commandment" 4:
You shall always look at the passage's surrounding setting.

■ Put each sentence in its immediate setting

(a) Romans 8.37

People have preached many sermons on this verse, stressing that we can have Christ's power to overcome our temptations and sins. But is that what Paul was talking about here? Discover the answer by looking at verses 35, 36, 38 and 39. What is Paul talking about?

....

....

....

Always look at the setting!

(b) "Avoid the passions of youth"
(2 Timothy 2.22a).

This "text" has often been used to urge Christian teenagers to stay sexually pure and unattached. But the setting shows that these are not the sort of passions that Paul was warning Timothy about.
Look carefully at:

(i) verses 23–25;
(ii) the rest of verse 22.

Now write in your own words what you think Paul was really telling Timothy not to do.

....

....

....

Remember "Commandment" 5:

You shall check whether the real meaning of a passage is what it seems at first sight to say.

Always look at the setting!

(c) 1 Peter 3.4

At a boys' Christian holiday party, one of the leaders rebuked a group of boys for being too rowdy, on the grounds that God wanted them to be quiet! To prove his point, he quoted this verse.

Look it up and from the surrounding verses decide whether you think he had really proved his point or not.

YES / NO

WHY? ....

....

Always look at the setting!

■ The setting can help you apply any Bible passage

Look up Revelation 3.20.
This is a very popular verse for people thinking about starting as Christians.

But look at the verse's setting, Revelation 3.14–22.
Do you think it is meant to be about making a start as a Christian?

YES / NO

WHY? ....

....

In the light of what you decide, apply verse 20 to your own life now:

F God/Jesus ....

....

AA ....

....

TA ....

....

Always look at the setting!

Always look at the setting

BLOCK 2: THE WIDER SETTING OF THE SECTION, THE BOOK AND THE AUTHOR

■ The section

(a) The lost (or prodigal) son

From memory, without opening a Bible, write down in a sentence what you think is the main point of this parable of Jesus.

....

....

Now look up Luke 15.1–3 to see who Jesus told his three "lost" parables to:

....

Imagine you are one of these original listeners; what was Jesus trying to say to *you* through the third parable?

....

....

....

Compare your answer now with what you wrote down before.

Always look at the setting!

(b) The wedding at Cana

Again, before looking the passage up, write down what main thing you think Jesus was trying to teach through his miracle of turning water into wine:

....

....

Now look up John 2.11 to see what Jesus in fact achieved through it (and presumably had mainly in mind).

....

....

How does this compare with what you wrote first? There were always secondary "spin-offs" from Jesus' words or actions; but you must start from his *main* point in order to make sense of them. The setting can often tell us this.

Always look at the setting!

■ The book

For example, John's Gospel and first letter.

(a) Look up John 20.30–31.
Complete the following in your own words:

The main purpose of John's Gospel is ....

....

Now look up 1 John 5.13.

The main purpose of John's first letter is ....

....

(b) Bearing in mind this knowledge of the *book's* purpose, and looking at the immediate setting as well, fill in the name of someone you know who would gain by understanding these verses (a different person for each verse; you may include yourself for one!):

John 3.16   ....

1 John 1.9   ....

John 14.6   ....

1 John 3.13   ....

Always remember the setting!

■ The author

(a) The Bible writers often describe things in terms of their interests or jobs, and this may influence what they choose to write about.

Even if you don't already know, can you work out from what you know of their interest or jobs, which of the following people said or wrote each of the following (i-v)?

JESUS   SOLOMON   PAUL   LUKE   DAVID

(i) My song is about loyalty and justice, and I sing it to you, O Lord.

(ii) Why do you look at the speck of sawdust in your brother's eye and pay no attention to the plank in your own eye? (NIV)

(iii) For we know that when this tent we live in – our body here on earth – is torn down, God will have a house in heaven for us to live in ...

(iv) I, the Teacher, was King over Israel in Jerusalem. I devoted myself to study and to explore by wisdom all that is done under heaven. (NIV)

(v) When Jesus saw her, he called out to her, "Woman, you are free from your illness!" He placed his hands on her and at once she straightened herself up and praised God.

(b) Read one of these passages and fill in a different word or phrase of your own to make clear exactly what the author seems to mean by "faith".

AUTHOR	PASSAGE	WHAT EXACTLY DOES HE MEAN BY "FAITH"?
Paul	Romans 4.13–25	....
James	James 2.14–26	....
Writer to Hebrews	Hebrews 10.35—11.2	....

Always remember the setting!

■ Session 4 ■

The basic method

AIM

This is really the central session of Ready to Serve. *We believe that to have a good, basic method to enable you to understand the Bible properly lies at the heart of being an effective servant of Jesus today. We explain here the one we consider best. The session is fairly solid, hard work, but the potential rewards are incalculable.*

All passages for study in this session come from the Sermon on the Mount. They are, of course, important passages to discuss in their own right; but the main aim of this session is to learn a method of personal study, not to hold a group discussion. Therefore it is essential to be ruthless in pushing on to the next item.

LEADER'S NOTES

BLOCK 1: THIS COULD BE THE MOST IMPORTANT HOUR OF YOUR LIFE!

1. Bible study methods

Sharing   5 mins

Divide people into small groups of three or four, but not more, and ask them to share together what system, if any, they use to shape their personal Bible study. If appropriate to your course members, encourage those who don't read the Bible on their own to say so, and to share what they find difficult about the idea; the others can perhaps reassure them from their experience. If you think the majority do not read the Bible on their own, do the same activity but relate it to private *prayer* rather than Bible study.

2. Method behind the madness

Study   25 mins

Sum up that some form of method is essential for getting things done. Explain that this series of sessions in *Ready to Serve* is building up a basic method for making sense of any passage you come across in the Bible. Stress that it is not the only method, but that it is reliable. People are welcome to prefer another, but we would like them to give this one a try. Part of the method involves always looking at the setting as in the last session, and the applications always and today of the one before.

So the next task is some revision from the last two sessions. Distribute to everyone a copy of page 122 from the members' pages. Item (a) involves sharing in the small groups you have formed. Allow about 3 minutes, then hear what answer one or two groups have reached, affirming them or improving them, as necessary. Item (b) likewise.

Item (c) begins with private study. After about 5 minutes, encourage the groups to share for another 5 minutes. It would be good if you could circulate round the groups at this point, to check that people are understanding the difference between the AA (sometimes very close to the actual words of the Bible) and the TA (something absolutely specific to learn or do within the next 24 hours).

Item (d) requires private study for about 4 minutes: hear one or two of the answers, affirming or refining them.

3. And now for this week's art appreciation spot

Study   15 mins

Announce that up to now you have covered only two-thirds of the basic method. (Allow pause for groans.) The other third is the same method as art teachers use in explaining a painting.

Display a reproduction of Holman Hunt's *The Light of the World*, and ask people to look at page 123. Work through (a), the description of *The Light of the World*, pointing out everything on the picture as you do so. Then look at the way (b) uses the same method with Matthew 6.24. Words or phrases in the Bible do not all carry the same weight. Each sentence or paragraph has a main subject; the remaining words are usually detail reinforcing that main point.

Ask the small groups to try this approach with Matthew 6.19–21 on page 124. As before, compare a couple of answers, to check that people are getting hold of the idea.

BLOCK 2: PUTTING IT ALL TOGETHER

1. Prayer and introduction

5 mins

We are now going to put the whole basic method together, and practise so that the group gets the hang of it. In the process, people will be studying teaching from Jesus that will challenge the way they live. So start this block by praying – either yourself, or ask one or two of the course members to lead in prayer.

2. The basic method

Study

30 mins

Page 125 of the members' pages shows one person's attempt to apply the basic method to Matthew 7.1–2. Look through it together as a full course to check whether you think this specimen follows the instructions (5 mins).

Then give everyone three copies of a blank, basic method sheet (page 126).

(a) Everyone should fill one sheet out for Matthew 7.12, trying to think how it applies to them *right now* (5 mins). They should then share their thoughts with the others in their small group (5 mins).

(b) Fill out another sheet for Matthew 7.7–8. For time's sake, do not share results (5 mins).

(c) The final practice passage is Matthew 7.24–27 (10 mins). Any who finish in time can compare answers, but tell people not to rush it.

It will be essential for you to circulate throughout this activity, offering help to all who find this analytical thinking difficult! Keep reminding them of the goal, which is to hear clearly what God is saying to them *today* through the Bible.

3. Review and prayer

10 mins

Ask everyone to look back over the basic method pages for 5 minutes, and select one thing they think God is telling them to do. The members of each small group should then share their findings and pray for each other.

LEADER'S NOTES

The basic method

BLOCK 1: THIS COULD BE THE MOST IMPORTANT HOUR OF YOUR LIFE!

■ Method behind the madness

REMEMBER: APPLICATION ALWAYS AND TODAY. ALWAYS LOOK AT THE SETTING!

(a) Work out the *fact* about God behind Matthew 6.1.

....

....

(b) Decide what sort of practical action Jesus means for an always application of Matthew 6.2–4.

....

....

(c) In your own words, write down what you see as the *fact* about God and the *application* to you, *always and today*, in Matthew 6.5–6.

F God ....

....

AA ....

....

TA ....

....

Share your answers with the rest of your group.

(d) Look through the whole of Matthew 6.1–15 and note any important points from the *setting* of this section of Jesus' sermon, which will enrich your understanding of the Lord's Prayer the next time you pray it:

....

....

....

....

■ And now for this week's art appreciation spot

(a) An art teacher

describes a painting: *The Light of the World* by Holman Hunt.

Main subject	Jesus holding a lantern, knocking at a door. (This is the *point* of the picture.)
What do the *details* add?	Dark night, thistles, weeds, fallen apples, no handle on door. (These add to the main subject, showing a dark, neglected, closed world which Jesus lights up.)
What does the *setting* add?	The frames and venues (St Paul's Cathedral and Keble College, Oxford) add to the majesty and spiritual challenge of the main subject.

(b) And the same with the Bible

Each passage or unit within a passage is a bit like a work of art. We can make sense of it in the same way. For example, Matthew 6.24.

Main subject	You cannot serve two masters – God and money (or materialism).
What do the *details* add?	You love whatever your god is, and hate whatever fights against it. If we truly belong to God, we should take a wary view of money.
What does the *setting* add?	In the verses immediately following, Jesus shows that he is talking about our attitude to daily needs: food, drink and clothes. We should rely on God for them more than on our bank balance.

TRY IT! In this grid, try the same approach with Matthew 6.19–21.

Making sense of the Bible, picture-style

Main subject	
What do the *details* add?	
What does the *setting* add? (Look up the verses before and after to see if they throw extra light on the main point.)	

SESSION 4

The basic method

BLOCK 2: PUTTING IT ALL TOGETHER

■ The basic method

Bible passage:
BOOK Matthew
CHAPTER 7
VERSE(S) 1–2

Fact about God
One way that God will judge our lives is by the standard we use to judge other people.

1

What is the fact about God or his will behind the main subject the speaker or writer meant for his listeners?

What does the setting – immediate and (or) wider – add to the main subject?

Setting
Parable of speck and plank means hypocritically finding fault with someone else, while blind to our own faults.

2

Details
I don't think that "Don't judge" means "*Never* assess or criticise other people" (because verses 2 and 5 imply that we should, but in the right spirit). It must be a very strong warning to be careful, fair and honest when we do.

3

What do the details – words and phrases – add to the main subject?

Main fact about God
Remember: each time I point out a weakness in someone else, God checks up on my life for the same weakness.

4

In the light of boxes 1–3, what do you now see as the main fact God means you to learn or do?

Always application
Check this habit I'm developing of knocking everything the minister does.

5

How should this affect the way you think or live in general?

Today application
When I talk to my wife this evening, *make sure* that everything I say about the minister is true, fair and kind – *especially* about lack of organization as that is *my* weakness too.

6

What action should you take as a result in the next 24 hours?

The Basic Method

Bible passage:
BOOK
CHAPTER
VERSE(S)

Fact about God

What is the fact about God or his will behind the main subject the speaker or writer meant for his listeners?

What does the setting – immediate and or wider – add to the main subject?

Setting

Details

What do the details – words and phrases – add to the main subject?

Main fact about God

In the light of boxes 1–3, what do you now see as the main fact God means you to learn or do?

Always application

How should this affect the way you think or live in general?

Today application

What action should you take as a result in the next 24 hours?

■ **Session 5** ■

Words, words, words!

AIM

This session concentrates on developing some of the skills associated with
square 3 of the basic method grid (see page 128). "What do the details add?"
will include individual words and phrases.

BLOCK 1: TRACKING DOWN THE MEANING

1. Humpty Dumpty and Alice

Reading   5 mins

Ask two good readers (in advance, if you think they
will need to practise), one male, one female, to read
the extract adapted from *Through the Looking-
Glass* (page 129). After the reading, comment that
if we want to make sense of the Bible, we cannot
treat its words Humpty Dumpty fashion!

2. A word game

5 mins

Divide the group into pairs and distribute copies of
page 130 from the members' pages. Tell them to go
through the list on their own, ticking the words
they understand, crossing the ones they don't.
Reassure people that there is no disgrace in not
knowing something.

After a minute make them swap books with their
partners. Partner A makes partner B explain for 2
minutes one or two of the words B has ticked. (If B
has not been able to tick any of the words, A should
explain some of B's crosses.)

Then reverse the process, with A explaining one
of her or his own ticks or one of B's crosses, again
for 2 minutes.

Check, briefly, how they got on; many people are
confused about the real meaning of words like "sin"
and "holy", so you may need to clear them up. But
you are only exposing the problem at this stage, so
there is no need to go into great detail or give
people more than one turn each at this activity.

3. Where do you go for help?

Check-list   5 mins

Move the pairs on to the next list (page 130). They
should first complete it on their own, then compare
their scale of priorities with their partner's.

Ask what came first with most people. Three
bonus points all round if "the setting" came near
the top of the list!

4. How the setting helps us find a word's meaning

Bible study   30 mins

Move on to the next activity (page 131). Work
through the first three passages together as a full
course. For what it is worth, our understanding of
the word "law" in these passages is:

John 19.7 – a particular rule binding on the Jews,
    perhaps one of God's commandments, e.g.
    Exodus 20.3,7; or Leviticus 24.16.

John 7.19 – the whole range of God's laws conveyed
    to the people through Moses, and contained in
    the first five books of the Bible.

John 12.34 – a name for the whole Old Testament.
    (The passages they were thinking of may have
    included Psalm 110.4; Isaiah 9.7; Ezekiel 37.25;
    Daniel 7.13–14.)

Then ask people to tackle Romans 10.4 in pairs or
small groups. Give them 5 minutes, then check to
see how well people have understood it. It should
be clear from the second half of the verse, and from

127

verses 2, 3 and 5–11, that "law" here means something like "trying to earn eternal life by keeping God's laws in the Old Testament".

For the last 15 minutes or so, ask people to apply Romans 10.4 to themselves, using the basic method. Provide copies of page 126.

BLOCK 2: CONCORDANCE – THE ROLLS-ROYCE OF WORD-TRACKERS

1. Why use a concordance?

Input   10 mins

Distribute copies of pages 132–135 from the members' pages. Read through the first section together.

Pass round any concordances you possess or can borrow. Pool ideas with your course members on where they can get access to one when they need it; and indeed, where they can buy one if they want to invest in this invaluable resource.

Point out that concordances come at three different levels of completeness and usefulness:

(a) "concise", as in some study Bibles;
(b) "complete", a full list of occurrences of all the main English words; for example, *Concordance to the Good News Bible*, The Bible Societies; *The NIV Complete Concordance*, Hodder and Stoughton.
(c) "analytical", which subdivides the words according to the words they translate in the original Hebrew or Greek. This is the most useful kind of concordance for Bible students.

2. How to use a concordance

Study   20 mins

Read through the four steps together, then let people work through the example at their own pace, with or without partners. Or you might prefer to do it orally as a full course. At the end, point out how the study made use of the concordance information.

3. How to find out what the Bible says on a subject people disagree about

Study   15 mins

If there is time, ask people to do the exercise on page 135–136, working out what the New Testament teaches about God's "wrath". Again they should work alone or with partners, as suits them best.

You will need to sum this up yourself with a short explanatory epilogue of your own. It would be ideal to leave time for discussion, but this may not be possible.

Advance warning

Session 6, Block 2 includes an exercise based on a Bible atlas. Ask course members to bring any that they own or can borrow.

Humpty Dumpty and Alice

Alice finds herself in a difficult conversation with Humpty Dumpty

A: What a beautiful belt you've got on! (*On second thoughts*) At least, a beautiful cravat, I should have said – no, a belt, I mean – (*in dismay*) oh, I *beg* your pardon!

H: (*after a pause*) It is a – *most – provoking* – thing, when a person doesn't know a cravat from a belt!

A: I know it's very ignorant of me.

H: It's a cravat, child, and a beautiful one, as you say. It's a present from the White King and Queen. There now!

A: Is it really?

H: They gave it to me for an un-birthday present.

A: (*puzzled*) I beg your pardon?

H: I'm not offended.

A: I mean, what *is* an un-birthday present?

H: A present given when it isn't your birthday, of course.

A: (*considers*) I like birthday presents best.

H: You don't know what you're talking about! How many days are there in a year?

A: Three hundred and sixty-five.

H: And how many birthdays have you?

A: One.

H: And if you take one from three hundred and sixty-five, what remains?

A: Three hundred and sixty-four, of course.

H: ... That shows that there are three hundred and sixty-four days when you might get un-birthday presents –

A: Certainly.

H: And only *one* for birthday presents, you know. There's glory for you!

A: I don't know what you mean by "glory".

H: (*contemptuously*) Of course you don't – till I tell you. I meant "there's a nice knock-down argument for you!"

A: But "glory" doesn't mean "a nice knock-down argument".

H: When *I* use a word, it means just what I choose it to mean – neither more nor less.

A: The question is, whether you *can* make words mean different things.

H: The question is, which is to be master – that's all. (*Pause*) They've a temper, some of them – particularly verbs, they're the proudest – adjectives you can do anything with, but not verbs – however, *I* can manage the whole lot! Impenetrability! That's what I say!

A: Would you tell me, please, what that means?

H: Now you talk like a reasonable child. I meant by "impenetrability" that we've had enough of that subject, and it would be just as well if you'd mention what you mean to do next, as I suppose you don't intend to stop here all the rest of your life.

Adapted from *Through the Looking-Glass, and what Alice Found There*, by Lewis Carroll. Published by Macmillan, 1871.

Words, words, words!

BLOCK 1: TRACKING DOWN THE MEANING

■ A word game

In the following list of Bible language, tick the words or phrases you understand, cross the ones you do not:

....	Christ	....	Salvation
....	In Christ	....	Repent
....	Messiah	....	Prophecy
....	Grace	....	Holy
....	Sin	....	Walk (or live) in the light

■ Where do you go for help?

List the following guides in order of value to you if you do not know a word in a Bible passage:

.... the Church minister

.... Whitaker's Almanack

.... the setting

.... English dictionary

.... another modern Bible translation

.... Clare Rayner

.... common sense

.... a Bible commentary

■ How the setting helps us find a word's meaning

The word "law" in the Bible can mean several different things; often it is obvious from the setting.

In John 19.7 it means ....

In John 7.19 it means ....

In John 12.34 it means ....

Now look up Romans 10.4 with one or two others.
Does "law" mean the same as in any of the three cases above?

YES/NO

If YES, which one ....

If NO, what *does* it mean? ....

....

Remember? Always look at the setting!

SESSION 5

Words, words, words!

BLOCK 2: CONCORDANCE – THE ROLLS-ROYCE OF WORD-TRACKERS

■ Why use a concordance?

An excellent way to get the most out of a Bible word or phrase – whether or not you already know what it means – is to look at (some of) the other places it is used. This will fill you in with an all-round picture of the Bible's teaching on that subject.

Remember "Commandment" 6:

You shall, where possible, use one part of the Bible to make sense of another.

To do this you need a concordance - a book listing every major word used in the Bible, and all the verses in which the word occurs.

■ How to use a concordance

(a) Look up the word you are studying. The concordance lists each word alphabetically.

(b) Look up each verse in the Bible listed under that word.

(c) Where you feel a verse is going to throw light on the word's meaning, stop and look carefully at the setting.

(d) Make a note of what you learn.

An example

Try this with the word "self-control".
Look at the section below, taken from a concordance. It lists all the GNB uses of "self-control" in the Bible.

Prov	5.23	He dies because he has no **self-control**.
Acts	24.25	discussing about goodness, **self-control**, and the coming Day of Judgement,
1 Cor	7.5	giving in to Satan's temptation because of your lack of **self-control**.
Gal	5.23	goodness, faithfulness, humility, and **self-control**.
1 Tim	3.2	he must have only one wife, be sober, **self-controlled**,
2 Tim	1.7	his Spirit fills us with power, love and **self-control**.

For **Ready to Serve** course use only © Bible Society 1995

Tit	1.8	He must be **self-controlled**, upright, holy, and disciplined.
	2.2	Instruct the older men to be sober, sensible, and **self-controlled**;
	2.5	husbands and children, to be **self-controlled** and pure,
	2.6	In the same way urge the young men to be **self-controlled**.
	2.12	and to live **self-controlled**, upright and godly lives
1 Pet	4.7	You must be **self-controlled** and alert, to be able to pray.
2 Pet	1.6	to your knowledge add **self-control**;
	1.6	to your **self-control** add endurance;

Now work on this summary of all the teaching they give.

(a) Look up *Proverbs 5.22–23*.

What happens to people with no self-control? ....

Do you think this is literally true, or poetic exaggeration?

....

What area of life does the setting (verses 15–21) show the writer is referring to?

....

Now put verses 22–23 into your own words to show exactly what you think they mean.

....

....

....

(b) Now look at the last sentence of *1 Corinthians 7.5* in its setting (verses 1–5). Again, put the sentence into your own blunt, direct, modern words to show exactly what kind of temptation and self-control you think Paul is talking about.

....

....

....

(c) If you were explaining the Christian faith to a friend who is not yet a Christian, what do you think would be the three words or topics you would talk most about?

....

....

....

Now look up *Acts 24.24–25*. What three themes did Paul "go on

discussing"? ....

Why do you think self-control was so important to him?

....

What (if anything) is good news about self-control?

....

(d) *Galatians 5.22–23 and 2 Timothy 1.7* tell us how Christians develop
self-control.
Some Christians today speak as if self-control and the Holy Spirit being in
control of our lives were opposites. Their slogan is "Let go [of your own
control] and let God [take over]". What do you think, in the light of these
verses, Paul might want to say to them?

....

....

....

(e) *1 Timothy 3.2 and Titus 1.7–8* show Paul demanding self-control as a
qualification for church leaders. How far do you think it should still be
required today? Why?

....

....

....

(f) *Titus 2.2, 5–6, 12* show Paul demanding self-control of *all* Christians, not just
leaders. What reason does he give (verse 5)?

....

....

How far do you think that reason still holds for Christians today? Why?

....

....

(g) Look up *1 Peter 4.7*.
How might being more self-controlled make you more able to pray?

....

....

....

(h) 2 Peter 1.5–7 lays out a set of good qualities for Christians to build on to their lives. How might you be able to add self-control to your faith, goodness and knowledge over the next week?

....

....

....

LOOKING BACK

How far has this concordance study changed your image and understanding of self-control?

....

....

....

■ How to find out what the Bible says on a subject people disagree about

The wrath or anger of God

Using the concordance approach, see what you can learn about this phrase. Many people dislike the idea of "wrath" or anger applied to God, but the concordance shows that it (and similar phrases) are used 580 times in the Bible; that is an average of about one every other page!

Remember "Commandment" 7:

   You shall not ignore the bits you don't like!

Other people feel that the wrath of God is an Old Testament idea, done away with in the New Testament by the love of God. Without trying to draw any conclusions at this stage, see what you can learn about God's anger (which GNB sometimes translates as "punishment") from the New Testament alone, from the following selection of passages.

(a) Romans 2.1–5 ....

....

....

(b) 1 Thessalonians 5.9 ....

....

....

    (c) Romans 5.8, 9..

        ....

        ....

    (d) John 3.36 ....

        ....

        ....

    (e) Ephesians 5.3–7 ....

        ....

        ....

■ **Session 6** ■

Inside information

AIM

This session explores the Bible's historical background, to help us get into the minds of the Bible's writers; to know more of how they felt and thought. The better we understand what God was saying through the Bible then, *the more accurately we will understand what he is saying through it* now.

BLOCK 1: WHY WE NEED INSIDE INFORMATION

1. How much information have you got inside you?

Quiz   10 mins

Distribute copies of pages 139–140 from the members' pages. This is a quiz seeking to demonstrate how much background knowledge we need, to make sense of many passages in the Bible. You may like to run it orally with your whole course, or to ask people to answer the questions in small groups or alone. Explain that it does not matter how well people do (though you could offer a light-hearted prize, if you like); urge them not to take it too solemnly, or get bogged down with rival explanations. But they will expect you to have done your homework, and be able to supply a reliable answer!

It is essential for you to sum up by stressing that the point of the activity is not for us all to be walking "Masterminds", but to show that to make full sense of the Bible, we need to understand the world the writers lived in and the way they thought. The further exercise at the end is valuable in showing that we often need this information if we are to apply Bible teaching to our lives today.

2. Cultural background

Study   10 mins

One obvious strand of this inside information is cultural background, i.e. the national customs at the time of writing, which are not the same for us.

Let people work on Mark 7.1–13 on pages 140–141 in small groups of three or four, for about 5 to 6 minutes. Then check whether they have made sense of "Corban". If not, read DBJ Campbell's explanation to them:

Despite the Fifth Commandment, a Jew could get out of the responsibility to support his parents by offering his money as a gift (*Corban*, in Aramaic) to the Temple. He could not then touch it in order to help his parents. It had become dedicated. "By Corban" was also an oath whereby a person swore by the gift or sacrifice on the Temple altar. If a Jew used such an oath, however thoughtlessly, when refusing to help his parents, the oath could not be broken. Thus, said Jesus, the Law of God could not be kept because the traditions over-ruled it. (*The Synoptic Gospels*, John Murray, p.74)

Encourage them to make any extra notes of this.

3. The reason for writing

Study   25 mins

Another vital area of inside information is knowing the author's reason for writing, particularly in the case of the New Testament Letters. The writers knew what they were talking about, and so did their first readers, but it is not always easy for us to piece this information together.

A good example of this is Colossians. Divide people into three groups. Give each group one of these passages from chapter 2:

(a) verses 8–10 and 20–23;

(b) verses 11–15;

(c) verses 16–19.

Each group should try to construct from its verses what the outsiders are saying to the Colossian church – the ideas that Paul and Timothy are trying to counter.

After 10 minutes compile the information you have deduced.

For the last 10 minutes or so of this block ask people to apply the main subject of Colossians 3.1–3 to themselves in the light of information discovered. Provide copies of page 126, for them to use the basic method.

BLOCK 2: HOW TO FIND INSIDE INFORMATION

Block 1 required you to scoop out the information with your fingernails. The good news is that you don't have to rely only on fingernails! In this block, we look at three vital tools for excavating the information we need. Try to have several examples of each on display – perhaps some for sale.

1. Bible atlas

Study and discussion   15 mins

Provide copies of the map on page 142 in the members' pages. Work all together on the questions about Jesus' and the disciples' mission-field in Matthew's Gospel (10 minutes). You may need to help people a little with activity (d). If your Bible translation does not use the term Decapolis, explain that it is a Greek name for an area of ten cities or towns. And point out that territory "on the other side of" the Jordan (Matthew 4.25) is viewed from where the story is taking place, i.e. Galilee (verse 23). Draw out of those who know them, the facts that all the regions except Galilee, Samaria and Judea were Gentile territory; and that God's "people of Israel" lived in Galilee where Jesus and his disciples were working.

Ask course members to show any Bible atlases that they own, and to explain how they use them. Compare notes on where you can borrow or buy them.

2. Commentary

Study and discussion   20 mins

Ask people to turn again to Colossians 2.8–23, and this time to read it alongside the commentary on page 143, alone or in pairs. The point of this is to see what the commentary adds to their understanding of the passage they studied in Block 1. After 10 minutes, stop to discuss this as a full course.

After a further 5 minutes, show any one-volume commentaries (or series of commentaries) that you would recommend. Share experiences of commentaries, good and not so good; and give advice on where people can borrow or buy them.

3. Bible dictionary and handbook

Study and discussion   10 mins

Ask people to pool their knowledge, in groups of five or six, of who or what the Pharisees were and did (2 mins).

Then ask a good reader to read aloud the extract from *The Lion Handbook to the Bible* on page 144. Ask the groups to look again at Mark 7.1–13, and compare thoughts on what the Handbook extract has added to their understanding of it.

Then show any Bible Dictionary or Handbook that you use; and share ideas among the course members where they might be able to borrow or buy others.

LEADER'S NOTES

SESSION 6
Inside information

BLOCK 1: WHY WE NEED INSIDE INFORMATION

■ How much information have you got inside you?

Test yourself by reading this passage from Matthew 10, and trying to answer the questions in the right-hand column. They all require background knowledge which Matthew does not supply here.

(a) Jesus called his twelve disciples together and gave them authority to drive out evil spirits and to heal every disease and every sickness.

Why 12 rather than, say, 8, 15 or 96?

(b) These are the names of the twelve apostles: first, Simon (called Peter) and his brother Andrew; James and his brother John, the sons of Zebedee;

Why called "apostles"?
Why called Peter?

(c) Philip and Bartholomew; Thomas and Matthew, the tax collector; James son of Alphaeus, and Thaddaeus;

Why draw attention to the tax collector?

(d) Simon the Patriot and Judas Iscariot, who betrayed Jesus.

What was a Patriot?
What does Iscariot mean?

(e) These twelve men were sent out by Jesus with the following instructions: "Do not go to any Gentile territory or any Samaritan towns.

Who were the Samaritans?

(f) Instead, you are to go to the lost sheep of the people of Israel.

Sheep? Literally?

(g) Go and preach, "The Kingdom of heaven is near!"

What is the Kingdom of heaven?

(h) Heal the sick, bring the dead back to life, heal those who suffer from dreaded skin diseases, and drive out demons. You have received without paying, so give without being paid.

Does he give these same commands to Christians today?

(i) Do not carry any gold, silver, or copper money in your pockets;

(j) do not carry a beggar's bag for the journey or an extra shirt or shoes or a stick. Workers should be given what they need.

How does this reason explain the instructions in the earlier sentence?

(k) When you come to a town or village, go in and look for someone who is willing to welcome you, and stay with him until you leave that place.

How do you know he will invite you?

(l) When you go into a house, say, "Peace be with you." If the people in that house welcome you, let your greeting of peace remain; but if they do not welcome you, then take back your greeting.

What does this verse mean?

(m) And if some home or town will not welcome you or listen to you, then leave that place and shake the dust off your feet.

What does this gesture mean?

(n) I assure you that on the Judgement Day God will show more mercy to the people of Sodom and Gomorrah than to the people of that town!

What Judgement Day?
Who or what were Sodom and Gomorrah?

Look through the questions again and tick those for which answers are *vital* in order to reach God's AA and TA of these instructions for *you*.

■ Cultural background

Look up Mark 7.1–13.
Because the Jewish religious laws and customs of Jesus' time were so different from anything we know today, it is difficult for us to make sense of this passage.

What two main customs does the story refer to?

(a) ....

(b) ....

In which verses does Mark try to explain the background for his readers?

....

But even so, he hasn't room to explain fully the "Corban" law (verse 11). Pool your knowledge to make sense of it.

....

....

....

....

....

Inside information

BLOCK 2: HOW TO FIND INSIDE INFORMATION

■ Bible atlas

This map can give us further insight into the passage we looked at in Block 1 – Jesus' instructions to the disciples (Matthew 10).

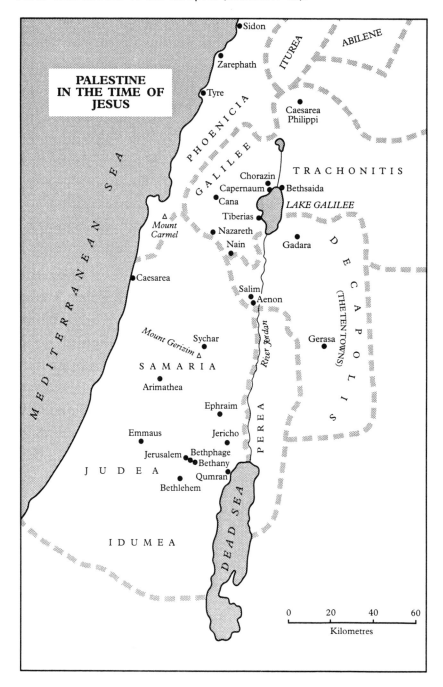

For **Ready to Serve** course use only © Bible Society 1995

(a) Jesus was based in Capernaum (Matthew 4.13; 8–5); this was his "own town" (Matthew 9.1). Find it on the map.

(b) From time to time he and his disciples crossed the lake by boat. One time they went to Gadara (Matthew 8.28); find it on the map. How far was the journey?

(c) Most of their teaching was in the towns and villages of Galilee (Matthew 4.23; 9.35). In Matthew 11.21 Jesus names the ones he visited most often apart from Capernaum; find them on the map.

(d) Crowds followed him from all the surrounding regions (Matthew 4.25); find them on the map. But he restricted his disciples' mission (Matthew 10.5–6). Work out from the map where they could and could not go.

■ Commentary

Paul hints that some person whom he could name was distorting truth (4), distortion which those steadfast (5), and rooted, and built up in Christ, and grateful for such blessing (6, 7) could undoubtedly withstand. "Beware lest someone be found to rob you, through the empty deceit of his philosophy, based on human tradition and the attitudes of the world – and not on Christ" (8). In Christ, who revealed God himself in such fulness as the mind could comprehend (9), they had all that God could give. He has no rival spiritual authority (10). The old Jewish rituals no longer had validity. Spiritually he fulfilled the old covenant (11). The death of the believer in Christ is death to sin (11, 12. Rom. 6. 10), to the law, and all ancient bondage (13–17). The battery of metaphor finds a climax in v. 14 which claims that Christ paid the debt, cancelled the written statement, nailing high in public exhibition the outdated document of obligation (14), and, like a Roman general on triumphant procession to the shrine of Capitoline Jupiter, he had led all oppressors chained and captive (15). Why, then, in folly fall again under the tyranny of their petty regulations (16), laws only framed to educate the uninformed until full truth should break on them in Christ (17)? And this freedom was a reward to hold. Let no petty theological despot, usurper, charlatan or concocter of strange doctrine cheat them of such treasure (18). The deceiver was in the church but failed to function as a part of that knit and active body (19). It was absurd for a member of Christ to function outside that unity (20), a slave to superseded rules and regulations (22).

From *Commentary on the New Testament* by EM Blaiklock, published by Hodder, © Edward England Books.

■ Bible dictionary or handbook

Parties, sects, and movements in Judaism

● **The Pharisees.** These were the religious purists—a party which grew from the 2nd century "Hasidim" (God's loyal ones) and concentrated on control of religious, rather than political, affairs. Their supreme concern and delight was to keep the law (including, of course, the traditions) in every exact detail. (Most scribes belonged to the Pharisee party.) Judged by this standard, they were model Jews (Philippians 3.5–6). To this end, they kept themselves as far as possible apart from other men: they could not eat with a non-Pharisee in case the food had not been tithed (i.e. one tenth given to God).

Inevitably, perhaps, this policy of separation led to disdain for all lesser mortals, a "holier-than-thou" attitude which has made their name a term of reproach today. This arrogance, combined with a dry legalism which put exact ritual observance before love and mercy, led them into conflict with Jesus. He did not dispute their orthodoxy, but the proud and unloving way in which they upheld it. The influence of the Pharisees was out of all proportion to their numbers, which were seldom large. It was the Pharisees who laid down the lines along which Judaism developed after the destruction of Jerusalem in AD 70. They ensured a continued emphasis on individual piety and strict ethical standards, as well as their better-known rigid legalism. They were respected, if not loved, by other Jews.

From *The Lion Handbook to the Bible*, article by Richard France, pages 494–5 reproduced by permission of Lion Publishing.

■ **Session 7** ■

Picture language, poetry and parables

AIM

In this final session we look at non-literal styles of writing, which are often misunderstood. We offer guidelines for making sense of picture language, poetry and parables. Practising on some examples in the session should make people confident to tackle similar passages on their own.

BLOCK 1: PICTURE LANGUAGE

1. Where does it come?

Quiz   5 mins

Provide copies of the quiz from page 148 of the members' pages and try the quiz, alone or in pairs.

Give them 2 to 3 minutes and then check the answers. We think there should be rings round psalms, parables, Revelation and prophecy (most OT prophecy is written as poetry). Not everything in these categories is picture language, and the history books and letters do contain some picture language. Poetry tends to use it much more than prose.

2. Making sense of picture language

Guided study   40 mins

Point out that we always use guidelines for understanding different kinds of writing, whether we realize it or not.

For instance, we don't read adverts in a newspaper as though they were the front page news report! In this section we look at some guidelines for making sense of picture language, which we can use in addition to all the other ways to make sense of the Bible we have already picked up (sessions 2–6). We don't repeat those lessons here, but they are necessary for making full sense of picture language.

Move on to the next section (pages 148–149) in the members' pages. You will be leading the whole course through this together.

(a) Ask people to do the first question (John 4.10–15), either orally with you, or in small groups. The point is to see that the woman mistakenly took Jesus' words literally, when his picture language pointed to something other than literal water.

So dictate or display on a board or an OHP rule no. 1 for making sense of picture language: **"Ask: should we take this passage literally and at face value? or is it a picture pointing to something else?"**
Give people time to write it down.

(b) Ask them to try this rule on John 21.15–17. We suggest that Jesus' question and Peter's answer about loving Jesus are literal; they mean just what they say at face value. But Jesus' instructions to look after his lambs and sheep are pictures used to point to something else.

A question which might occur to people is, "How can I *know* what is meant to be literal and what pictorial?" This brings us to rule no. 2: **"Take a passage literally unless there are good reasons to believe it is picture language."**

These good reasons will mainly be what you pick up from the setting (session 3) and from "inside information" (session 6) on the passage. Here, for example, there are two good reasons to think that Jesus didn't have a flock of real sheep and lambs:

(i) A flock of sheep belonging to Jesus isn't referred to anywhere in the NT; we know that Jesus was a carpenter by trade. He said that he

LEADER'S NOTES

had nowhere to "lay his head", let alone house a flock of sheep!

(ii) "Sheep" is a common OT picture for God's people and Jesus often used OT picture language in his teaching.

Move on to Mark 10.46–52. Let people think about the question and suggest their own answers before you sum up.

Healing miracles of this kind are favourites of a certain sort of preacher for "preaching the Gospel". While we agree that every new Christian's experience has parallels with that of Bartimaeus (e.g. we need to ask Jesus for mercy and help; he hears us and has mercy; he heals all Christians at some level of their personality), we see no good reason to understand this passage as directly stating those truths, or as a picture of them. So rule no. 2 guides us to take it as a literal account of something Jesus said and did to one person.

(c) Move on to Revelation 16.15. Ask for suggested answers to the questions, then sum up. It seems clear that the only way Jesus compares himself to a thief is in his coming unexpectedly; hence the advice to "stay awake". The picture is not intended to teach that Jesus steals things or

breaks the law (obviously that would go right against the rest of the Bible!).

These thoughts should help people formulate rule no. 3. Ask for suggestions before telling or showing it: **"Picture language normally makes only one point. Look for that and don't press the picture too far."**

The quiz on 1 Peter 2.4–5 gives a chance to try out this rule.

Clearly Peter does say we are living parts of the new fellowship whose purpose is to worship God. He tells us that we become part of this human "worship centre" when we come to Christ. The other three thoughts, while they may be true, are not part of what Peter is saying here.

3. A further example

Study   10 mins

You may need all the time available for activity 2 above, and it is important that you should not rush it. But if you have time to spare, suggest that people look on in 1 Peter 2 to verses 6–8, the further references to a stone. They should use the three rules of making sense of picture language to try to work out what Peter means. It is not necessary to look up the OT passages that he quotes.

BLOCK 2: POETRY AND PARABLES

Everything covered in Block 1 has a bearing on Block 2. Poetry contains much picture language, and Jesus' parables are a form of it. The further guidelines set out in this block are extra helps for making sense of what God is saying to us through poetry and parables. You will again be guiding the whole course through much of this block together.

1. Poetry in the Bible

Input and study   15 mins

(a) Provide copies of page 150 from the members' pages. Explain that poetry is another major part of the Bible: it accounts for one-third of the Old Testament and parts of the New Testament. It does not rhyme, but usually joins two "parallel" phrases, which have a close connection, one after the other.

   Work through the three common forms of parallelism all together. As you look up Psalm 34, show how the GNB and NIV lay out the lines which belong together:

– The first line of a pair starts at the left-hand margin.

– The second line (and sometimes a third parallel line, though for the sake of simplicity we are assuming only two here) is indented by about two letters.

– The remainder of any line which is too long to fit in, is carried on underneath, indented by about five letters.

(b) Ask people to do the questions on Psalm 34.5, 8 in pairs, unless they prefer working alone. This version of the psalm is from the NIV translation, as the GNB translation puts the picture language in a simpler form.

   After 5 minutes, go quickly through the exercise together, asking for the suggestions people wrote down. Add any comments you need to.

   Both verses seem to us to be examples of type (i) parallelism: the two phrases mean exactly the same thing. This helps us to understand the picture language. The second phrase determines the meaning of its parallel.

In verse 5, those who look to the Lord for help are "radiant" (not, as some have suggested, because they reflect the beauty of the Lord they are looking at), but because he prevents them being put to shame or disgraced by their enemies (second line). You could point out the setting, given in the psalm's heading, just before verse 1. David has just escaped from mortal danger at the hands of the Philistine king, Abimelech. So his "radiance" is the joy of freedom.

In verse 8, the "taste" is not, as some have taught, a forecast of the Communion service, but (from the second line) the personal experience of taking refuge in the Lord, i.e. trusting him for protection, and finding him trustworthy.

2. Making sense of parables

Guided study   30 mins

Move on to the next section (page 151). In this activity we are thinking about Jesus' famous parables, and not the wider use of the word "parable" in the Bible.

(a) Work through this section fairly quickly all together, taking answers out loud. Augustine's mistake was to try to find a separate meaning for each detail in the story.

So dictate or display rule no. 1 for making sense of parables: **"Look for the main point of the story."**

It seems that the main point of the parable of the good Samaritan was to show the lawyer that he couldn't choose who he would love; his neighbour was anyone in distress that he might meet.

(b) But the main point of this parable obviously has not exhausted all it can teach us. Ask people what else they think Jesus means us to learn from it.

So rule no. 2 is: **"Look for any minor points the story may also be making."**

Let people work alone or in pairs for 3 to 4 minutes on the first question about the

parable of the gold coins. Then hear one or two answers, and sum up. Here the setting seems to show that Jesus' main point in telling the story was to warn the disciples, excited by his revolutionary dealings with the chief tax collectors, that his final coming as King was further off than they thought.

Again, let people work for a few minutes on the second question before you take soundings and sum up. There are probably many minor points, which should not bear the same weight in our application as the main point. We are aware of the following:

(i) Before Jesus comes again as King, there is work for his disciples to do; we should use the gifts God has given us in serving him.

(ii) Many people who say that Jesus is their Lord, do not live as if he really is.

(iii) Those who obey and serve him will be used even more in his service; those who stagnate spiritually will lose the opportunities they once had.

(c) As with section (a), work orally all together. We understand the error here to be reading into the parable a great deal more than it says. No example story can possibly reflect every aspect of a major Bible doctrine.

So rule no. 3 is: **"Don't press the details too far – certainly not to contradict the rest of the Bible!"**

3. Applying a parable

Bible study   10 mins

Again, you may have run out of time while working on activity 2, and it will have been time well spent. But if you have time in hand: *either* ask people to return to the parable of the gold coins (Luke 19.11–27) and to apply the main point to themselves, using the basic method; *or* (longer) turn them to the parable of the workers in the vineyard (Matthew 20.1–16). First, they should use the three rules for making sense of the parable, then apply the main point to themselves – with the basic method. In either case, provide copies of page 126.

Picture language, poetry and parables

BLOCK 1: PICTURE LANGUAGE

■ Where does it come?

Here are some of the broad types of writing we find in the Bible. Ring the ones which you think are likely to contain a great deal of "picture language" (for example, poetry, illustrations, made-up stories), rather than straight talking or reporting:

history   psalms   prophecy

parables   letters

Revelation (the last book of Bible)

■ Making sense of picture language

(a) Look up John 4.10–15.
What was wrong with the Samaritan woman's attempt to make sense of what Jesus was saying?

....

....

Rule No. 1 for making sense of picture language:

....

....

(b) Look up John 21.15–17.
Mark L against any of these sayings you think are meant to be taken literally; mark P against any you think are meant to be picture language:

"Do you love me?"
"You know that I love you."
"Take care of my lambs."
"Take care of my sheep."

Rule No. 2 for making sense of picture language:

....

....

Look up Mark 10.46–52.
Many preachers take this kind of story as a picture of how we become
Christians. "We are spiritually blind and can only ask God for mercy. But
then we meet Jesus and he has mercy on us, etc." Do you think it is meant
to be pictorial in this way?

YES/NO

WHY? ....

....

(c) Look up Revelation 16.15.
These are words of Jesus, talking about his second coming. In what ways
does Jesus say that he *is* like a thief?

....

....

In what ways is Jesus *not* like a thief?

....

....

....

Rule No. 3 for making sense of picture language:

....

....

Look up 1 Peter 2.4–5.
Tick which of these ideas (all suggested in a recent discussion) really come
from the picture in this verse:

☐　　　　　every Christian is like a living stone;

☐　　　　　so we all ought to be solid characters;

☐　　　　　Jesus wants to build Christians together into
　　　　　　a glorious fellowship, worshipping God;

☐　　　　　the cement that holds us together is love;

☐　　　　　if we are in close fellowship, we can protect
　　　　　　each other from the wind of life's storms.

SESSION 7

Picture language, poetry and parables

BLOCK 2: POETRY AND PARABLES

■ Poetry in the Bible

(a) Bible poetry usually consists of sentences made up of two lines which are parallel in their meaning. There are three common forms of this parallelism (and the third can be subdivided again):

  (i) The two phrases mean exactly the same thing (for example, Psalm 34.3).

  (ii) The second is the opposite of the first (for example, Psalm 34.10).

  (iii) The second adds to the first –

    a) explaining it (for example, Psalm 34.16);

    b) telling the consequence or next step (for example, Psalm 34.19).

(b) Now use the parallelism to help you make sense of complete verses. Often, the second half of the verse helps to throw light on the precise meaning of the first.

For example, Psalm 34.5 (NIV)

"Those who look to him are radiant;
their faces are never covered with shame."

Which kind of parallelism is this?

In what sense are those who look to God "radiant", and why?
Use the second half of the parallel to help answer this question *in your own words.*

....

....

Psalm 34.8 (NIV)

"Taste and see that the LORD is good;
blessed is the man who takes refuge in him."

Which kind of parallelism is this?

For **Ready to Serve** course use only © Bible Society 1995

How do we "taste" God? Use the second half of the parallel to answer *in your own words.*

....

....

■ Making sense of parables

(a) St Augustine (AD 354–430) was a famous scholar who tried to make sense of the parable of the good Samaritan (Luke 10.25–37) by using the following "key".

the man	– Adam
the thieves	– the devil and his angels
the priest and Levite	– the Old Testament
the Samaritan	– Jesus
the inn	– the Church
the innkeeper	– the apostle Paul

Do you think he got it right? if not, where did he go wrong?

....

....

Rule No. 1 for making sense of parables:

....

From Luke 10.27–29 and 36, what is the main point of the story of the good Samaritan?

....

....

(b) What else do you think Jesus means us to learn from the story of the good Samaritan?

....

....

....

Rule No. 2 for making sense of parables:

....

Look up Luke 19.11–27, the parable of the gold coins. What is the main point of the story? (Bear in mind verses 7–10 and 11.)

....

....

What minor points do you think the story is also making?

....

....

....

....

(c) Look up Luke 15.11–24, the parable of the lost son.
What is wrong with the following understanding of the parable? "The Father accepts the son back without any sacrifice; *therefore* the idea that Jesus had to die on the cross before God could forgive us is wrong."

....

....

Rule No. 3 for making sense of parables:

....

....

Remember "Commandment" 8:
You shall not over-emphasize one truth out of proportion, so that it contradicts something else in the Bible.

Something to do at home

We strongly recommend that you do some further work at home between sessions of this series. This will help you go on thinking about the course, and begin to put what you are learning into practice.

■ (A) Basic level

Your leader will help you choose one or more of these options.

After session No. 1

YOU CAN DO IT!

1. (a) Read slowly and steadily through Psalm 119. List the rewards it promises those who meditate wholeheartedly on scripture.

   (b) Apply one or more of the "Ten commandments for making sense of the Bible" to your regular reading of the Bible this week.

   (c) Script a conversation between you and a brand-new Christian who says, "Don't ask me to read the Bible; I could never make head or tail of it."

   (d) "Set book": study a passage with special attention to the "Ten commandments for making sense of the Bible".

After session No. 2

WHY DO PEOPLE THINK THE BIBLE'S BORING?

(a) Continue practising with several Bible sentences: list the F, and your AA and TA.

(b) Take special care to *apply* your regular Bible reading personally all this week.

(c) Write a set of notes for home-group leaders in your church or area to help them answer people who say, "I used to read the Bible, but I gave up because it was so boring".

(d) "Set book": follow the procedure of (a) and or (b) with selected passages.

After session No. 3

ALWAYS LOOK AT THE SETTING

(a) Continue practising with several Bible sentences and longer passages; answer these two questions about their setting:

(i) what does the immediate setting add to my understanding of this passage?

(ii) what does the wider setting (section, book, author) add, if anything?

(b) Always look at the setting, immediate and wider, in your regular Bible reading this week.

(c) Write an introduction for your next group Bible study, or for some future occasion, explaining how the setting of section, book and author help you to understand the passage you will be looking at.

(d) "Set book": follow the procedure of (a) and or (b) with appropriate passages.

After session No. 4

THE BASIC METHOD

Try working in pairs or threes if it helps you get the hang of the basic method.

(a) Continue using the basic method on any Bible sentences or passages that you have been thinking about recently.

(b) Try applying the basic method to a key verse or sentence in your regular Bible reading at least one day this week.

(c) Write a letter to the course leader, honestly expressing your feelings about the basic method at this stage.

(d) "Set book": use the basic method with selected sentences or passages.

After session No. 5

WORDS, WORDS, WORDS!

(a) Borrow or buy a concordance, and look up all references to the word "conscience". Plan the outline of a short talk to teenagers (your youth fellowship or local school Christian Union) on the Bible's teaching about conscience.

(b) Use the same approach for some other important Bible words, for example grace, faith, life, death, peace.

(c) Try a concordance study of at least one key word in your regular Bible reading this week.

(d) Try applying the basic method to some key verses connected with your Christian discipleship, for example from the passage in your group Bible study, Sunday service or child's church group, etc.

(e) "Set book": use a concordance to trace the Bible's teaching on some of the more important or difficult words in the book.

After session No. 6

INSIDE INFORMATION

(a) A child asks you, "What's a Sadducee?" With the help of a Bible dictionary, write down the answer you would give.

(b) Borrow or buy a Bible dictionary and atlas, to use the same approach with other Bible words, places or people. For example, covenant, circumcision, tabernacle, scribe, Sinai, Sodom and Gomorrah, Babylon, Herod, Pharaoh.

(c) In your regular Bible reading this week make a point of grappling with anything you instinctively disagree with or don't understand. Use concordance, atlas, commentary or Bible dictionary, as appropriate.

(d) "Set book": use these same resources to get to grips with some important words and phrases in the book, which you can only understand with inside information on historical background.

After session No. 7

PICTURE LANGUAGE, POETRY AND PARABLES

(a) Use the basic method with:
   (i) John 15.1–11;
   (ii) Psalm 23;
   (iii) The parable of the good Samaritan (Luke 10.30–36).
   In each case decide what is the main point or key sentence to focus on.

(b) Apply the relevant rules of making sense of parables and picture language to some harder passages:
   (i) Revelation 4;
   (ii) Ecclesiastes 12;
   (iii) The parable of the shrewd manager (Luke 16.1–9).
   Get as far as you can before calling on outside help!

(c) Prepare a speech to take part in a debate on: "Song of Songs – Solomon's sex-drive or spiritual love of God?" Decide which you think is the right way to make sense of this book, and defend it.

(d) "Set book": use the relevant rules and the basic method with any passages using picture language.

■ (B) Advanced level

After session No. 1

YOU CAN DO IT!

Read Matthew 3. Make a note of any parts you don't fully understand at first reading. Review the "Ten commandments for making sense of the Bible" and put as many of them as you can into practice. For each one that helps you, write down how it prompts you to look at something in this passage in a new light. (Later sessions will explain the commandments more fully, and show how they can be more helpful still.)

After session No. 2

WHY DO PEOPLE THINK THE BIBLE'S BORING?

Read Matthew 4. Work out what God is saying to you – go through the process F–AA–TA – through verses 4, 7,10,17,19 and 20.

After session No. 3

ALWAYS LOOK AT THE SETTING

Read Matthew 8 and 9 straight through. Then look at each incident in the two chapters in turn, and write down any extra understanding you gain through concentrating on their setting – think how your impression of Jesus grows from one section to the next. And reflect on what you know about Matthew the author; what would particularly interest him as he chose and recorded these incidents?

After session No. 4

THE BASIC METHOD

Read Matthew 5. Then practise the basic method on each of the following verses: 3,4,5,6,7,8,9,10–12,13.

After session No. 5

WORDS, WORDS, WORDS!

Read Matthew 12:1–14. Look up the Old Testament passages Jesus refers to. Then sum up in your own words his teaching in this passage about the Sabbath, and its relevance to your life today. Then use a concordance to see whether Jesus adds any further teaching about the Sabbath elsewhere.

After session No. 6

INSIDE INFORMATION

Read Matthew 12.22–45, and sum up in your own words Jesus' teaching in this passage about demon-possession and its relevance to your life today. Use any "inside information" helps that you need.

After session No. 7

PICTURE LANGUAGE, POETRY AND PARABLES

Read Matthew 13:1–23. Use the three rules of making sense of parables on the parable of the sower. Then use the passage as a guide for a letter you write to a young Christian friend who has asked you, "Why did Jesus give so much of his teaching in parables, instead of 'telling it straight?'"

Finding the job God wants me to do in my Church

Introduction

Aim

This series of seven sessions forms a basic introduction to the skills required for being an active servant of Jesus Christ in your church. It goes through only the first steps of Christian ministry, and does *not* qualify anyone to be a psychiatrist or a world-famous Christian speaker. It seeks to help people reach a clearer idea of the job God wants them to do in their church; and should point the way forward to opportunities for further training in a specialist area.

By taking in the series title of "the job God wants me to do *in my church*", we do not mean that people's Christian service is confined to helping other church members. Some jobs, such as leading a home group or children's club, may well be, but others in this series, such as helping other people and telling them about Jesus, often happen in other settings. But we still regard these as church-based work: Christian service that should be recognized, supported and cared for by the Christian fellowship you belong to.

Content

The topics for the seven sessions are:
1. Leading a group meeting: Bible study
2. Leading a group meeting: prayer time
3. Helping other people: understanding
4. Helping other people: listening and responding
5. Outreach: telling people about Jesus
6. Speaking in public
7. What job *does* God want me to do in my church?

The sessions have been designed to run in this sequence. If you leave some sessions out or change the order, you will need to adapt some of the activities in them.

Core groups

Groups of four people are the basic working unit throughout this series. If you have an odd number of course members, have one group of three. If you have an even number that does not divide into four (e.g. 10,14), have one group of six – do not leave a couple on their own.

We recommend that you keep the membership of these small groups constant, so that people build a strong relationship of trust and support, in which to practise the various skills in each session. It is an extra strong reason for urging course members to make the seven sessions of this series top priority. If one of them really cannot come, the group can continue as a three. But if numbers drop to two, the group should join another one.

By all means plan who should be in which group yourself. Try to make sure that you have at least one reasonably mature, experienced Christian in each group. You will need them to encourage others through the thinking, sharing and experimenting with new skills.

"Something to do at home"

There is only one level of assignments in this series (members' pages 220–221), but most contain elements of choice. All involve doing something to practise the ideas and skills explored in the previous session. They also ask for some written work; this is not essential, but it is a valuable discipline in itself, and it is a useful way to check the quality of someone's work if you plan to award a certificate. However, these assignments are only suggestions; if they are not suitable to your circumstances, replace them with something more relevant.

■ Session 1 ■

Leading a group meeting: Bible study

AIM

Block 1 takes the first steps in forming the small core groups, which will be the basic working units throughout Series 3. (See section 3 of the Introduction on page 159.) They should make an ideal subgroup within your course of just a few people for each member to get to know better, and support through the first steps of Christian service. There should be four in each group, but if the numbers don't quite fit, allow one group of three, five or six.

As for subject matter, this session and the next look at two aspects of leading home Bible study or fellowship groups. These are the obvious skills to learn about at the same time as forming groups. Block 2 of this session focuses on leading group Bible study. Not all your members will be suitably gifted to be permanent group leaders, but, if they are members of a group, it should be valuable for them all to be able to take a turn at leading Bible study from time to time.

Obviously, there is no point in doing Block 2 of this session if your church has no Bible study groups, and if your course members have no other involvement with them. In that case, use only Block 1 from this session. Follow it with Block 1 of Session 3 or one of the other sessions that better fit the needs and opportunities in your church.

BLOCK 1: GROUP-FORMING

1. Take your partners

(a) *Thanks for the memory*

25 mins

(7 mins)

Divide people into pairs who are likely to work well together. They will form part of the core groups who will stay together throughout Series 3. Ask each person to jot down happy memories or achievements at various ages on members' page 163, and then share this information with their partner. It is a good way of getting to know each other a little better, and of showing how they have developed as people.

(b) *Four facts – one fake!*

(6 mins)

People should now complete the sentences under "Four facts, one fake!" on page 163 alone.

Then ask them to share these facts with their partners, who try to guess the trick one. It is a good way to build up their knowledge and understanding of each other.

(c) *Personal scavenger hunt*

(12 mins)

Now arrange people in groups of four, by bringing together two pairs. These should be the core groups who will work together for the rest of the series. See the introductions to Series 3 and Session 1 for what to do about odd numbers. Explain that they will be working together over the next few sessions. They have the chance to help each other as Christians and as church members. This will involve supporting and caring for each other.

Ask them to start by each telling the "new" pair one fact they have discovered about their partner in the previous two activities.

Now they are to get to know each other a little more! They should hunt through their clothes, pockets, handbags or wallets for the following items:

(i)   an old keepsake;
(ii) something useful;
(iii) a source of comfort.

Each should show (i) and suggest what it reveals about them. If the others see anything else significant or typical in the item, they should say so. Then go round a second time with (ii) and so on. Tell them to keep it moving briskly, and get as far as they can in the time.

2. What are you doing in this church?

Group-building   15 mins

After meeting each other, we now turn people to the part they play in your church fellowship. By the end of Series 3, they may well want to change, deepen or increase their contribution; but for the moment they should only think about their present involvement.

Activity (a) on page 164 is an interesting way to express their role within church life, as they see it. If they found themselves locked out of the building one Sunday, how would they react? Like one of the figures in the picture, or in another way? In (b) they should list the form or forms their commitment to the church fellowship and its ministry takes. In (c) they should look ahead to how the core group might be able to help them over the next few weeks. They can do this on page 165, "Welcome to the core group".

Let people fill in their own answers for 5 minutes, then share them with the group. Tell the groups to note what each member hopes the others might do for them over the next few weeks. It will then be up to them to make sure it happens!

3. Welcome to the core group

Reflection   5 mins

Finish the block with everyone working alone on the rest of page 165. But do not rush the group actvity 2(c) above. If your time has gone, ask people to do the rest of "Welcome to the core group" at home later.

BLOCK 2: PRESENTING AND PREPARING

1. Presenting group Bible study

Input   20 mins

Ask if anyone can remember taking part in a particularly helpful group Bible study. If any can, ask one or two of them to explain what exactly was so good about it. Can you draw any conclusions from their experience about the main purposes of group Bible study?

Now provide and look all together at pages 166–167 from the members' pages. The five tips there flow from the main purpose of group Bible studies at All Souls', Langham Place, where this course originated. Compare this with the way you as a church see the aim of any Bible study groups you have. Fill in your church's aim if it is different. Then look through the tips and, if necessary, change them and add to them to fit *your* aim. Discuss any comments or questions that arise from the tips which you agree.

Obviously, if your church already produces written instructions for Bible study leaders, it will be more helpful to look at those. If it doesn't, you might like to produce a revised edition of pages 166–168 to use in your church.

If this first activity proves valuable and takes all your time, don't worry. You could well set activity 2 below as something to do at home.

2. Preparing group Bible study

Input   25 mins

Look through the suggested programme together on pages 167–168. Explain that this is only one basic approach to leading Bible study; there are many others. But we recommend that people give this one a try. It helps to start with one workable method, which you can later develop.

At step b ask course members to suggest one or two sample passages from each section of the Bible that *would* be suitable for group study.

As you look at steps d to g, consult the study outline on pages 171–173 as an example of what they mean.

For practice, ask people to work alone or in pairs, on preparing steps d to g with Mark 10.35–45. It does not matter how far they get in the time. Be available yourself to give help and advice.

Leading a group meeting: Bible study

BLOCK 1: GROUP-FORMING

■ Take your partners

(a) Thanks for the memory

Jot down two happy memories, perhaps a much-loved pet or present, or achievements (for example, something you made or won) from each of these age-periods:

7–12	....	....
13–17	....	....
18–23 the last 3 years	....	....

Now share them with your working partner. What do they show of the way your interests and concerns have developed?

(b) Four facts – one fake!

Complete the following sentences, but deliberately make one statement wrong as a trick. Don't make it too obvious – your partner is going to have to guess which one is the fake!

My favourite game as a child was ....

My favourite subject at school when I was 12 was ....

My favourite music when I was 15 was ....

My favourite leisure activity now is ....

Now share these with your partner and see if they can spot the fake. When they have guessed, tell them the right answer.

■ What are you doing in this Church?

Taken from Pip Wilson's *Spectacular Stinking Rolling Magazine Book*. © 1991 Pip Wilson and Ian Long, published by Marshall Pickering an imprint of Harper Collins Publishers Limited.

(a) Where do you see yourself in this picture? (Circle one of the blob-characters.) If you don't think you are one of them, add yourself to the picture by drawing another.

(b) How would you describe your job or contribution to your church at the moment? (For example, member of Sunday congregation, member of home-group, coffee-maker, assistant treasurer, etc.)

....

(c) How might this "core group" help you play your part better in the church fellowship? (Tick any of these answers that fit.)

- [ ] Take an interest in me.
- [ ] Listen to me.
- [ ] Lend me a hand.
- [ ] Lend me a book.
- [ ] Lend me something else.
- [ ] Tell me to get a move on.
- [ ] Tell me to cheer up.
- [ ] Give me a pat on the back.
- [ ] Give me a kick in the pants.
- [ ] Tell me about themselves.
- [ ] Read the Bible with me.
- [ ] Pray for me.
- [ ] Something else: ....

■ Welcome to the core group

Write down the names of the other members of your core group.
Beside each one, note:

(a) the way each member hopes the rest of you might help them during the
rest of the course.

(b) one other new thing you have learned about them through this session.

Pray for them for a few moments.

Leading a group meeting: Bible study

BLOCK 2: PRESENTING AND PREPARING

■ Presenting group Bible study

Five tips for the group leader

These tips stem from the All Souls', Langham Place, aim for group Bible studies: **to help the group members discover God's truth for themselves.**

What are your church's aims for group Bible studies?

....

....

....

In the light of your aims, should you change these tips or add others? If so, agree the changes together.

(a) TALK AS LITTLE AS POSSIBLE
Don't give a sermon, but get the group to do most of the talking. You only need to speak to make sure the journey of discovery is still moving in a helpful direction.
Try never to make statements, always to ask questions.

(b) REFUSE TO ANSWER QUESTIONS YOURSELF
Many group members, especially young Christians, will ask questions about a Bible passage, but do not become the "guru" handing them answers on a plate. Make them study the passage themselves, either by passing the question on to the group ("What do others think about that?"), or by referring it back to the questioner ("What are your own ideas on it?")

(c) STICK TO THE PASSAGE YOU ARE LOOKING AT
Do not parade your knowledge of Old Testament verses and other Bible passages on the same subject. The group members will feel overawed, and that it's obviously not worth thinking for themselves.
    Do not allow discussions to wander too far off the point. You can always stop red herrings with "Let's discuss that question over coffee afterwards"; or, if you know the person well, "Which verse do you get that from?!"

For **Ready to Serve** course use only © Bible Society 1995

(d) LEAD, DON'T BE LED

If a Bible study turns into a boring, rambling discussion, it's often the leader's fault. You may need to protect all the other members from one or two who talk too much or get sidetracked. You are there to *lead*: quietly and gently you may have to axe a particular line of conversation, and move on to another subject. Or you may have to take a talkative person aside, before or after you meet, and ask them to hold back to give quieter group members the chance to contribute.

(e) BE READY TO LET THE CONVERSATION CUT INTO NEW CHANNELS

Don't stifle new insights on the passage, just because you didn't notice them first. All group members have a right to contribute. But keep control of the conversation.

Other tips?

■ Preparing group Bible study

A programme to guide you

(a) PRAY

2 mins minimum

Ask God to give you the wisdom and skill to help people discover his truth for themselves.

(b) CHOOSE A SUITABLE PASSAGE (if one is not set for you)

5 mins

Not all passages are suitable for group study.

It is best to be quite short: NT Letters – about 7 or 8 verses;

Gospels – about 10 to 12 verses;

OT – about 10 to 20 verses.

And it needs to make at least five separate points worth discussing.

(c) STUDY THE PASSAGE FOR YOURSELF

30 mins

Enjoy it, let it speak to you, master it. (Use the basic method learned in Series 2.) Use a commentary to help you understand it, but don't quote it or refer to it during the group study for fear of making the discussion academic and theoretical rather than about daily life. Check the passage in the other Bible versions that members bring.

(d) DIVIDE THE PASSAGE INTO MANAGEABLE SECTIONS

5 mins

About 4 to 6 verses is the maximum you can concentrate on at once. Divide the passage into suitable sections following either the paragraphing in your Bible, or the sense of the passage. Give each section a heading.

(e) PREPARE QUESTIONS TO OPEN UP DISCUSSION ON THE PASSAGE

20 mins

(a) *Never* pose questions that are too difficult or too easy (for example, which demand a simple yes or no answer). Good questions often begin: what, when, who, why, how?

(b) Begin each section with one general question (GQ), to which there are several possible answers.

(c) Devise further questions to each possible answer to the GQ, to draw out more fully the *meaning* (FQ-M) and *application* (FQ–A) of each phrase or verse you discuss. Be ready to adapt the A questions to follow on from the answers you get to the M questions.

(d) Have plenty of A questions, and be ready to go on and on asking them. Don't give up a subject till someone has been down-to-earth and personal about how we should react to what God is saying.

(f) ALLOW A BALANCED PART OF THE TIME FOR EACH SECTION

5 mins

If some verses are more important than others, spend more time on them. Don't let the group spend all the time on details that are not important. When your time is up for one section, move on, however little of it you may have discussed.

(g) PREPARE A BRIEF INTRODUCTION

5 mins

You may need to explain how the study will operate, or what the setting of the passage is; or tell people how God has used the passage to teach you something. But "KISS" (**K**eep **I**t **S**hort, **S**tupid!) or you'll make them clam up.

(h) PRAY again!

3 mins

■ Session 2 ■

Leading a group meeting: prayer time

AIM

This session continues the development of group-life begun in session 1. The skill it instructs in is leading a prayer time as part of a home-group meeting.

BLOCK 1: GROUP-BUILDING

Activity 2 assumes that your course members have done home assignment (b) or (d), preparing a group Bible study. If not, you will have to devise alternative activities, or spend longer on Block 2.

Two people in each core group will have a chance to lead part of what they have prepared. It would be advisable for you or some other experienced assessor to check through the notes of some of the others, to make sure they are on the right lines.

1. Fun and games

(a) Group charades

10 mins

(5 mins)

You need to prepare in advance a stock of name tags for each core group. The names can be well-known characters, from fact or fiction (e.g. Lady Godiva, Oliver Twist, Charlie Chaplin, Paul Daniels, members of the royal family). The tags should have adhesive backs or safety pins to stick quickly on the people's backs.

Ask everyone to gather in the core groups. One person stands in the middle of each group and receives a name tag on their back. The others silently mime the character on the tag till the person in the middle guesses it. Then someone else has a turn.

(b) One frog ...

(5 mins)

Now the core groups are to experience working together as a team. The aim is to do something enjoyable, but slightly testing, against the clock.

Go round the group with each member saying the next phrase of the riddle:

> One frog – two eyes – four legs – in the pond – kerplunk – kerplunk.

When it comes to two frogs, the next person must get the correct quantity of eyes, the next the correct quantity of legs. After that, you need one "in the pond" and two "kerplunks" for each frog. So it will run:

> Two frogs – four eyes – eight legs – in the pond – in the pond – kerplunk – kerplunk – kerplunk – kerplunk.

And so on. Count up to five complete frogs. If you make a mistake, start again.

The first group to finish cheers. Perhaps let two groups finish, but do not prolong the agony after that!

2. Group Bible studies

35 mins

In the groups, choose one person to lead a 10-minute study of part of the prepared passage. After 10 minutes ask the others to comment constructively to the leader on how they think she or he got on. Which parts worked well? Any suggestions for doing it even better next time?

Now choose another leader in each group. This time brief the others to play:

(a) someone who talks too much;

(b) someone who makes general comments, but never applies them to daily life;

(c) someone who keeps following red herrings.

The leader now leads them in a 10-minute study of the prepared passage, and deals as best they can with these "awkward customers". These awkward group members should resist the temptation to over-act, and should try to be realistically awkward! They should also come to heel when bidden! Circulate round the groups yourself, restoring order!

After 10 minutes ask the role players, back in their own characters, to comment constructively on how the leader got on, how he or she coped with the group, and how he or she might have done better.

For the last few minutes, share ideas on how to handle difficult members of groups. Reassure the leaders that in real life they would know the members of the group in advance and would have some idea of how to get the best from them.

BLOCK 2: THE PRAYER TIME

1. How to lead a prayer time

Input   30 mins

Distribute copies of members' pages 174–181. Explain that this is "programmed learning", seeking to make sure that you master and remember the main points. Once again, this is just one approach to a group prayer time; there are plenty of others. But this includes a great deal of wise experience and advice, and makes a good method to start from.

People should work through each section of the input, alone or in pairs, at their own speed, getting as far as they can in the time. They can finish it at home.

Spend a few minutes with each person or pair, checking that they are making progress. Answer any questions or add comments of your own.

2. Let's pray

Prayer   15 mins

Hold a prayer time in the core groups. Ask them to follow the outline on page 181.

In each group appoint someone as leader who has not yet led in this session. Tell them to keep the sharing short and simple, as they have only got 15 minutes, all told.

SESSION 2

Leading a group meeting: prayer time

BLOCK 1: GROUP-BUILDING

■ Group Bible studies

SAMPLE OUTLINE ON LUKE 11.1–13
(For reference or use in the home assignment after session 1.)

Key
GQ – General Question

FQ – Further Questions (to follow someone's answer):

–M – Question on the Meaning of the Bible words

–A – Question on the Application of the Bible words to our lives

Introduction: We all find prayer difficult. And yet we would all like to pray better. This passage of the Bible gives us Jesus' teaching on prayer. We know it almost too well and pass over it quickly. But it is full of helpful tips, so let's look at it carefully.

(a) *The ingredients of prayer:* verses 1–4 (half the available time)

The wording used in Church liturgy varies slightly from that used in the GNB.

GQ: What are the key features of Jesus' model prayer and how can we include these same ingredients in our own prayers?

Ans: *Father*
(Possible key feature 1)

FQ–M: Do you think this would have struck them as a surprising way to begin a prayer? Why (not)?

–A: How does calling God "Father" help us in our prayers?
Has it ever meant a great deal to anyone here?
When?

Ans: *Hallowed be your name*
(Possible key feature 2)

FQ–M: What does "hallowed" mean?

–A: How can we, in our prayers, treat his name as holy?
What have people found helps them to praise? (Adapt questions to M answers.)
How could we make our group prayer time more full of praise?

Ans: *Your kingdom come*
(Possible key feature 3)

FQ–M: What do we mean when we pray for God's kingdom?

-A: What can we do to ensure that God is definitely King in our lives?
       Is there anything we can do to extend God's rule in our society, or even
       other societies?

Ans: *Give us each day our daily bread*

(Possible key feature 4)

FQ–M: What do you understand by "daily bread"?

-A: What practical things might we be tempted *not* to ask God for? Why?
       Has that happened to you?

OR – Is it harder for us to rely totally on God in a world where so many
       things are produced by machines? In what ways is it harder?
       What do you find helps you to rely on God again?

Ans: *Forgive us our sins*

(Possible key feature 5)

FQ–A: Do you find that confession is a regular part of your prayer life? In
       what ways?
       Let's share some of our thoughts on this: why is it a regular part of
       your prayer life (or why not)?
       What is its value?

-M: Why does he add that we forgive others? What is the connection
       between forgiving others and being forgiven ourselves?

-A: Supposing we haven't really forgiven another person?
       What can we do about it?

Ans: *Lead us not into temptation*

(Possible key feature 6)

FQ–M: This is a strange prayer: would God ever lead us into temptation? Why
       (not)?
       Why should we pray against something which God might want us to face?
       Does Jesus' own experience in Gethsemane throw any light on this, if
       he prayed to be spared his trials?

-A: Do we fear temptation? What sort?
       How can prayer help?

(b) Teaching about God answering prayer: verses 5–13 (the other half of the time)

Introduction: Verse 9 is a tremendous promise - nothing can take that away.
But it sounds like a blank cheque – as if we can milk God for anything.

GQ: What does Jesus suggest in the surrounding verses 5–13 that *we* need
       to do or be, if God is going to answer our prayers?

Ans: *Friends with God* (5)

FQ–M: Who are God's friends?
       Does God answer the prayers of people who are not Christians?
       What extra confidence does the Christian have?

-A: How does it help you in prayer to know God as your friend?

Ans: *Wanting to help others* (6)

FQ–M: What sort of help might you be wanting to give to someone you are
       praying for?

Does this mean that God will only answer our prayers for *other* people?

    –A: How does this give you confidence in, say, praying for friends to become Christians and talking to them about Jesus?

  Ans: *Persistence* (8)

FQ-M: What does it mean to be persistent in prayer?

          Why do we have to be persistent? Why doesn't God answer immediately?

    –A: Are there any people or things you find it particularly hard to keep praying for? How could we help ourselves?

  Ans: *"everything you need"* (8)

FQ-A: If God gives us all we need, how does that affect our attitude to things?

          Can you give examples of things you feel less need of since being a Christian?

  Ans: *Seek* (9)

FQ-M: Do you think Jesus means anything different by "seeking" from "asking" or "knocking"? If so, in what ways do we need to "seek" in prayer?

    –A: How can I seek God's will about something that is not clear in the Bible? Has anyone had this experience of seeking God's will in prayer and gradually discovering it?

  Ans: *Trust* (11–13)

          Why do we find trust so difficult?

FQ-A: What can help us trust God to hear and answer as we pray?

Leading a group meeting: prayer time

BLOCK 2: THE PRAYER TIME

■ How to lead a prayer time

(a) Goals

At the end of this session you should be able to:

(1) state two basic aims of a prayer time, and distinguish between them;

(2) follow a pattern which will achieve both aims;

(3) understand four ways of helping a prayer time spring to life;

(4) find a storehouse of practical tips for using these helps.

(b) Input

(1) Many groups follow Bible study with a prayer time.
Suggest a reason why:

....

....

(2) There are two basic aims for a group prayer time:

    (i) to "pray in" the truths discovered during Bible study;
    (ii) to pray for each other's needs and concerns.

How does your answer to (1) above compare?

(3) Tick which you consider good reasons for a prayer time to follow group
Bible study:

(a) We have always done it this way.
(b) If God has spoken, we should respond.
(c) It is right to close a meeting in prayer.
(d) It is a restful end to the evening.
(e) Prayer for the other group members helps them in their problems.
(f) By praying, group members express their care for each other.

(4) Basic aim (i) is to "pray in" the truths you have discovered.
Some ways we may need to speak back to God are:

(a) thanking him for the truths he has shown us;

(b) asking for help to work out in daily living the applications we have thought of.

Can you suggest others? ....

....

....

(5) Basic aim (ii) is ....

(Check your answer with section (2) above.)

You will discover each other's needs and concerns by:

(a) listening to comments during the Bible study;

(b) a time of sharing news.

How does Paul describe this sharing of each other's concerns, in Galatians 6.2?

....

(6) The two basic aims are very different:

(i) is praying mainly for yourself;

(ii) is praying for others.

So it is probably best, but not essential, to divide the prayer time into two sections:

(i) "praying in" your response to the Bible study;

(ii) praying for ....

(7) If you do not divide the prayer time into two sections, basic aim (i) usually gets squeezed out, because:

(a) group members' needs seem so pressing;

(b) the lessons of the Bible study are already receding in the memory.

But basic aim (i) is important, because it develops the habit of speaking back to God when he has spoken to us.

(8) Can you think of any time you've been in a prayer session that has not gone well, and has seemed dead?

There are at least four ways of helping the prayer time spring to life:

(i) explanation;

(ii) example;

(iii) leading;

(iv) the Holy Spirit's help.

(9) Help (i): Explanation

Beginners can feel very nervous about praying out loud in their own words; the more you explain, the more you put them at ease.

What aspects of a prayer time might be helpful to explain?

....

....

....

....

Compare your ideas with sections (10) and (11) below.

(10) Explain **what you are going to pray about**.

For example, "If anything has struck you this evening, turn it into a simple prayer that God will make it real in your life; you may want to ask him for something, or praise him, or confess something."

It helps to give an example: perhaps along the lines of, "For instance, if you found the first verse helpful, you could quote it so we know what sparked off your prayer: 'The Lord is my shepherd'. And then pray very simply: "Thank you, Lord, that you care and look after us like a shepherd. Amen.'"

Similarly with sharing needs and concerns: for example, "Let's do what we normally do at this point and share news: things to praise God for and also things we could pray for as a group – maybe concerns at work or home, or friends who are ill or not Christians, and so on."

(11) Explain **how you are going to pray**.
Prayer is an art to learn. At each meeting explain one (probably not more) of these points:

(a) **From the Bible**
As you are aiming to "pray in" the Bible truths you have discovered, encourage people to keep their Bibles open.

(b) **For each other**
The joy of group prayer is to hear someone else praying for things on **your** heart; so encourage people to pray for others' needs, not their own (which they can pray for at other times).

(c) **Aloud**
It can be a great encouragement to others to *hear* someone praying for them. So invite people who feel comfortable to do so, to take their courage in both hands, and pray a simple prayer – it doesn't matter how short.

(d) **For one thing at a time**
You can kill a prayer time by praying in one prayer for all the needs that have been mentioned! Each member can pray several times, but stick to one topic at a time.

(e) **For some things in depth**

Some deep needs require more than one prayer: several people praying for different aspects of it, perhaps for a total of several minutes. When someone prays for the subject on the tip of your tongue, don't feel "She's pinched my prayer", but "Ah, someone else with my interest. Let's get really involved in praying for it." Be sensitive to the flow of the group's conversation with Jesus.

(f) **Briefly**

We don't have to impress God by going on for a long time and using complicated words. Keep prayers short and crisp, so that everyone can concentrate. Sometimes it is good to ask for prayers not longer than one sentence, or even just one name or need. (This can be specially good with praise, which some people find hard to keep up for more than a few words.)

(g) **With a time limit**

It is liberating to know how much time you have. If you give yourselves a limit of perhaps ten minutes or so, you can settle down, with that amount of time blocked off in your mind.

(h) **Announce who will start and who will finish**

Let people know where they are; don't leave long unexplained silences.

(12) Recap:

Help (i) is ....

Help (ii) is ....

(Check with section (8) above.)

(13) Help (ii): Example

Habits of prayer are more caught than taught.

As leader, you can do a lot to help the prayer time, simply by the *example* of how you pray. When you have explained how the group is going to pray, you must practise what you preach. So your own prayers should be:

(a) ....   (d) ....

(b) ....   (e) ....

(c) ....   (f) ....

(Check with section (11) above.)

(14) In particular, you set the tone by *your opening prayer*.

People will follow your example, not your instructions.

There are four golden rules for opening prayers:

(a) **Keep it brief**

Less than a minute, just a sentence or two.

(b) **Avoid "churchy" language that new Christians won't understand**

Some people relapse into quaint old-fashioned language when they pray. But God is our Father and our conversation with him should be as natural and simple as possible. Check yourself from using words and expressions that only long-standing Christians are likely to understand.

(c) **Keep to one subject**

A closing prayer can mention a number of subjects which no-one has prayed for, but the opening prayer should *not* embrace several topics at once.

(d) **Try starting with praise**

Thus you (i) stop the session becoming a shopping list;

(ii) show proper gratitude to our amazingly generous God;

(iii) build up the group's faith by getting them to focus on God's greatness.

(15) You also contribute helpfully with *your later prayers*. Here are five helpful tips for each separate prayer:

(a) **Quote Bible promises**

Perhaps part of a verse before or during your prayer. So you pray in response to God's word, and in line with it.

(b) **Home in on a subject**

Follow someone else's prayer with another on the same topic if it is important. Don't repeat or "correct" the first prayer, but take up another side of the toplc.

(c) **Be definite**

Why is the prayer, "Lord, make next Sunday's services a great success", less helpful than "Lord, prevent any buzz in the PA system"?

(d) **Be enthusiastic**

If you are excited with the privilege of prayer, the others will perk up too.

(e) **Don't hog the prayer time**

Give others a chance!

Allow good silences for them to summon up the courage to speak.

(16) Recap:

Help (i) is ....

Help (ii) is ....

Help (iii) is ....

(Check with section (8) above.)

For **Ready to Serve** course use only © Bible Society 1995

(17) Help (iii): Leading

You are the leader; therefore lead. Prayer times need leading, as much as Bible studies. You are not usurping the Holy Spirit; he will use you.

(18) Lead **during the time of sharing.**

(a) **Be prepared to butt in.**

People sometimes "share" for longer than is necessary – interrupt them: "And what exactly do you want us to pray for, Jean?"

(b) **Be prepared to question further.**

Some people say too little – find out more: "Could you tell us a bit more about how it happened?"

(c) **Share your own needs.**

Be honest and open about your own failures and needs for help.

(d) **Draw out the non-sharers.**

If you sense they are holding back only through lack of boldness, say: "Have you anything you'd like us to pray for, James, or any encouragement we could give thanks for?" If he pauses, you can prompt in possible areas of concern : "How are things at work, for instance?"

(e) **Encourage thanksgiving.**

Don't focus only on needs and problems. Ask for any answers to prayer and other causes for praise as well.

(19) Lead **during the time of prayer.**

(a) **By arranging a pattern of prayer.**

For example, pray in a circle, passing a Bible round: when you hold the Bible, you can pray; if you don't want to pray aloud, simply pass the Bible on.

(b) **By putting in a word to guide the praying.**

Sense the way the Holy Spirit is leading the prayer conversation. Then say, for example:

"Now let's move on from praise."

or "Perhaps two or three people could lead us in prayers of confession."

This is especially helpful when people

● **have lost track of what they should be praying for.**

● **are wandering off the subject** – so you might say something like: "Let's concentrate another moment or two on Sarah's operation."

● **are staying too long on a subject** – you might say; "Now let's move on to pray for other people, such as Joan's mother or Margaret's boyfriend."

(c) **By knowing when to stop.**

Be sensitive to the less enthusiastic in the group, who might get bored. It is often helpful to finish with the Grace or the Lord's Prayer, so that silent members can catch a sound of their own voice praying in public.

(20) Recap:

Help (i) is ....

Help (ii) is ....

Help (iii) is ....

Help (iv) is ....

(Check with section (8) above.)

(21) Help (iv): The Holy Spirit

The Holy Spirit will help you if you trust him to do so.
Pray for the prayer time in your preparation.
The prayer time is only a "success" when the Holy Spirit is present and
in control, stirring, encouraging, giving faith as the group prays.

(c) Quiz

Test how far you have reached the goals for this session. Try to fill in the spaces
without, at this stage, referring back to the earlier sections.

(1) (a) State two basic aims of a prayer time:

(i) ....

(ii) ....

(b) Point out the difference between the two aims:

....

....

(2) What pattern for the prayer time will ensure that you achieve those two
aims?

....

....

(3) List four ways for a leader to help a prayer time spring to life:

(i) ....

(ii) ....

(iii) ....

(iv) ....

(4) (a) Suggest two aspects of a prayer time which you could helpfully explain beforehand:

   (i) ....

   (ii) ....

(b) Name two golden rules for opening prayers which set a good example:

   (i) ....

   (ii) ....

(c) Suggest two stages of a prayer time when you can help by giving a definite lead:

   (i) ....

   (ii) ....

Check your answers with the previous pages.
Question (1) refers to sections (2) and (6).
Question (2) refers to sections (6) and (7).
Question (3) refers to section (8).
Question (4) refers to sections (10), (11), (14), (18) and (19).

■ Let's pray

Share two prayer requests with your group:

(a) the main need of a friend of yours (who can remain anonymous);
(b) one need of your own.

Then pray together, simply and briefly.

■ Session 3 ■

Helping other people: understanding

AIM

A third strand of belonging to a fellowship group, after Bible study and prayer, is to care for each other. Simple, caring help forms the next two-session theme in this series. This session aims at the first stage of helping others: understanding them. But the process we use is to help course members understand themselves, and then communicate their self-understanding to each other. The better we understand ourselves, the more we are likely to understand other people.

BLOCK 1: FAMILY BACKGROUND

Thinking about ourselves and our home background can be quite upsetting for some people. Be on the lookout yourself for anyone needing encouragement or reassurance, and alert any assistant leaders or mature Christians with a gift for caring.

1. Heroes and heroines

Sharing   10 mins

Explain that helping other people is basic to all forms of Christian ministry and that it therefore forms the next two-session theme in this series. It would be good to start with a prayer for God to meet *our* needs, so that we can then help meet others' needs.

Explain that this session will contain several simple activities to help people understand how they became the people they are now. First of all, point out that we can tell a lot about a person by finding out who they admire and want to be like. Then ask everyone to complete the "Heroes" survey from the members' pages, page 185.

They should then compare notes with one partner from their core groups (have a threesome if the core group is an odd number). Each should explain what the heroes or heroines reveal about their own development as people.

2. Your relationship with your parents

Sharing   15 mins

Move on to the next exercise, still in the same pairs. Explain that our parents and childhood have an immense influence on our character and attitudes. The more we know about someone's relationship with their parents, the better we will understand them.

We need to recognize that some people have less than ideal relationships with their parents, and some of their memories will be painful. But the influence of their parents in shaping the kind of people they are now is very strong. Explain this, and tell people any unhappy memory or experience of your own, if it is relevant. Encourage people to tell their partner anything *they want to*, but *no more* than they want to. Ask partners to be very gentle and sympathetic.

Some people, of course, scarcely know their real parents. The word "parents" here stands for whoever in fact brought them up as children (grandparents, step-parents, foster parents, etc.!)

Tell people to be quiet for a few minutes and think about their parents before doing the drawings. Encourage any who find drawing difficult or unnatural, by suggesting that they simply express their feelings in splashes of colour or a few key words. Provide some coloured pens.

When they are ready, ask people to talk about the drawings to their partners. Allow up to 5 minutes for each person to talk; some won't want as long as this, but some may and they should not feel rushed or cut short.

3. Your family crest

Sharing 10 mins

Except in core groups with only three members, swap people round, so that everyone works with another partner from their group. Ask everyone to move on to the "family crest" on page 186; to fill in their own "quarterings" and "motto"; and then show and explain it to their partner.

4. How do you see yourself?

Sharing 10 mins

The list on page 187 is a series of contrasts. Ask everyone to fill in for themselves, and then compare answers with their partner. If people find this approach difficult, give them an example: "Scottish Highlands" suggests a rugged, outdoors, "wide-open-spaces" kind of person; while "Caribbean Island" suggests a luxurious, sunbathing, "give-your-self-a-treat" kind of person. "Goalkeeper" is defensive; while "striker" is aggressive. And so on.

They should try to explain why they see themselves in these ways; and especially how their home or family background has made them that kind of person.

The block may have stirred deep feelings for some people. Announce that you (and anyone else suitable) are available to talk with anyone who feels upset.

BLOCK 2: SELF-IMAGE

This block helps all the course members to compare themselves with St Paul's view of himself as a mature Christian. We assume that at this early stage of working together, they will move through the activities fairly quickly and lightly. Encourage any who want to talk at greater length and depth to carry on afterwards, perhaps with you personally.

1. How you think of yourself

Bible study 30 mins

The core groups should gather again. For just a minute or two, each member should tell the others which *one* of all the different items in the "How do you see yourself?" list on page 187 of the members' pages they are most like. There is no need for any comment; but they or their partner from the end of Block 1 may put in a word of explanation if they want to. Keep it short, though!

Then ask everyone to move on to the Block 2 material on pages 188–189. Ask a good reader to read aloud the introduction and the passage from Philippians 3 and 4; then everyone should fill in their scores on the scales. The descriptions below the numbers are the extreme positions at the −5 and +5 ends of the scale. People need to judge where they come now between those extremes.

The point is to look at our basic opinion of ourselves, and to see how this affects our attitude to life's challenges. If the emphasis on *self*-image sounds rather self-indulgent and unchristian to anyone, explain that as with St Paul, the more Jesus-centred we are, the better understanding of ourselves we have; and the more we understand and accept ourselves, the more we shall understand and accept others. This will make us more like Jesus – more loving and generous.

After 5 minutes, ask members to share their answers in the core groups. They should help each other to explain why they feel as they do. Home and family background will be part of the reason; but so will things that have happened more recently. How far does their faith in Jesus help them? Look in on each group yourself for a few minutes; be alert for anybody giving themselves really low scores. Offer the chance to talk with you at the end of the session, rather than prolonging this activity now.

2. Understanding someone else

Guided meditation 10 mins

Tell everyone to think of someone else they know well (it could be another course member or somebody quite different, Christian or not). They should take a few minutes to look back over the scales on page 188–189. This time mark the scores they think this other person would give themselves.

Then tell them to reflect on *why* that person thinks of themself that way. Is it mainly family background, or more recent circumstances? Does Christian faith play any part?

After several minutes they should share any thoughts or findings with their core group. There is no need to tell anyone the name of the person they were thinking of, if they want to keep it private.

3. The core group revisited

Reflection   5 mins

For the last few minutes, people should turn back to page 165 from session 1. Beside the name of each member of their core group, they should note one thing they have come to understand better as a result of this session. Finish with a few moments for silent prayer and thanksgiving.

At the end, remind people that you are available to help anyone who would like to talk.

Helping other people: understanding

BLOCK 1: FAMILY BACKGROUND

■ Heroes and heroines

You can tell a lot about a person by finding out who they admire.
Write down the name of your hero(ine):

- at age 7–12 ....

- at age 13–17 ....

- at age 18–21 ....

- now ....

Now compare notes with the member of your core group you are working
with. Try to see how your different heroes reveal the way you have developed
in what you admire and think important.

■ Your relationship with your parents

Our parents and childhood have a big influence on who we are and the way we
think. In the boxes draw two pictures, diagrams, shapes or splashes of colour:

(a) to illustrate how you saw the relationship between you and your parents
when you were a child (for example, "mother hen and chicks", "bomb
under backside", etc.! Or perhaps draw some incident that happened);

(b) to illustrate your relationship with them now (or, if they have died, as you
last remember them).

Explain your drawings and talk about the memories they bring back.

■ Your family crest

Your quarterings

In the quarters put a word or a picture to express:

(a) An important quality you think you have inherited from your mother.

(b) An important quality you think you have inherited from your father.

(c) An important quality or concern you think you gained from your childhood family life.

(d) An important quality or concern you think you gained from your teenage years.

Your motto

Along the top of the shield, write a short saying or quotation to sum up your outlook on life now.

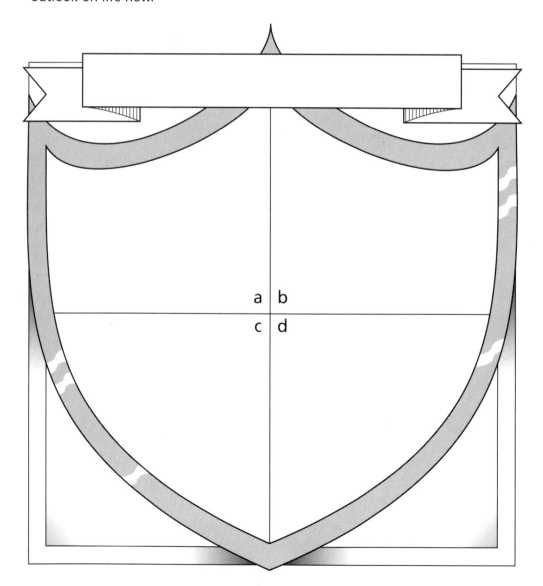

For **Ready to Serve** course use only © Bible Society 1995

■ How do you see yourself?

I think I am more like a .... than a ....

Circle the one on each line that you think you are *more* like:

bull in a china shop	wily fox
cultured pearl	rough diamond
deep mysterious ocean	babbling brook
Scottish Highlands	Caribbean Island
goalkeeper	striker
bursting sunflower	shy violet
taxi	push bike
mother hen	wild eagle

Helping other people: understanding

BLOCK 2: SELF-IMAGE

■ How you think of yourself

The apostle Paul clearly had a very stable, balanced self-image. But this was not self-centred; it was rooted in God's love. Because God loved him, he felt worth something; because Jesus was with him, he felt secure; because God had called him to follow Jesus, he felt able to keep moving forwards. He was in prison, likely to be put to death, yet he wrote to the Christians in Philippi:

> I keep striving to win the prize for which Christ Jesus has already won me to himself. Of course, my brothers and sisters, I really do not think that I have already won it; the one thing I do, however, is to forget what is behind me and do my best to reach what is ahead . . . I have learnt to be satisfied with what I have. I know what it is to be in need and what it is to have more than enough. I have learnt this secret, so that anywhere, at any time, I am content, whether I am full or hungry, whether I have too much or too little. I have the strength to face all conditions by the power that Christ gives me.
> Philippians 3.12b–14; 4.11b–13

Personal reaction

(a) Circle a number on each of these scales to show where your attitude comes between the two extremes.

(i) About the past I feel:

-5 -4 -3 -2 -1 0 1 2 3 4 5

trapped and   able to forget
haunted   what is behind

(ii) About the present I feel:

-5 -4 -3 -2 -1 0 1 2 3 4 5

frustrated   content in any and
and unhappy   every situation

(iii) About the future I feel:

-5 -4 -3 -2 -1 0 1 2 3 4 5

anxious and   I press on towards
hopeless   the goal

(b) Circle a number on these scales to show where you rate your self-image between the extremes.

SELF-HATE   **SELF-ESTEEM**

–5 –4 –3 –2 –1 0 1 2 3 4 5

(I am not OK. God blundered when he made me. I will never be any good.)   (God doesn't make mistakes. I *am* a valuable person, because he made me. Nothing can change that!)

SELF-PITY   **SELF-ACCEPTANCE**

–5 –4 –3 –2 –1 0 1 2 3 4 5

(I'm not clever, good-looking or good at anything. Nobody loves me.)   (Whatever my weaknesses, I am a whole person. God has given me all the equipment I need to live his kind of life.)

SELF-DOUBT   **SELF-CONFIDENCE**

–5 –4 –3 –2 –1 0 1 2 3 4 5

(I don't want to try, because I know I'll fail. I'll never make it.)   (I can do anything God wants me to, because he gives the strength. Failure only makes me try harder.)

As you share these answers with your core group, try to think what has happened in your life to make you feel the way you do about yourself.

■ Session 4 ■

Helping other people: listening and responding

AIM

Session 3 introduced understanding ourselves as a basis for understanding other people. A further vital ingredient of understanding other people in order to help them, is learning to be a better listener.

Once again, the experience of trying to help each other may unearth upsetting memories for some course members. Be on the lookout to help any who show signs of distress, and alert any other experienced helpers available.

BLOCK 1: LISTENING

1. Why listening?

Brainstorm   5 mins

Why do we start this session with "listening" as the primary practical skill involved in helping other people? Ask people to suggest reasons why the art of listening is so valuable; do not comment on people's suggestions, simply record them on a board or OHP. Let this brainstorm run for 3 minutes. If you think people may be shy of voicing their ideas immediately in front of everyone else, let them discuss the question for a couple of minutes in pairs, before reporting back.

If the following important points do not emerge, you should add them yourself:

● listening shows you really care;
● listening allows people with problems to express themselves;
● listening allows people to release and deal with their feelings;
● listening is the only way to understand the problem.

When the brainstorm is finished, read Proverbs 18.13 as a text for this session:

"Listen before you answer. If you don't you are being stupid and insulting."

2. Watching listening happen

Role play   20 mins

This is a structured role play to allow guided observation. Two or three experienced members of the course, probably including yourself, should meet before the session, to plan at least the outline of the following conversation, if not to script it word-for-word.

The advantage of three people is that you are trying to demonstrate good listening and bad listening. In that case, two of you are trying to help the other, who is extremely depressed by the domestic problem caused by mother-in-law living with the family; one of you listens well, the other badly. Try to ensure that your conversation will include at least one example of all the points on page 193.

In the session, ask everyone to turn to page 193 and try to observe each of the points in the demonstration conversation. When they observe something, they should make a note on the page to remind them later what it was.

The role play should take about 5 minutes. Then ask people, in their core groups, to discuss the three main sections on page 193, for about 5 minutes each. They should comment not only on the role play but on any other pieces of advice or

LEADER'S NOTES

experience they can offer on distress signals, good ways to listen and blockages to listening.

3. Just listen

Sharing 20 mins

Explain that during the rest of the session you will at some stage ask three people in each core group to talk about *something they don't mind sharing*. Stress that no-one should feel pushed into saying more than they want. You want them to share whatever they think appropriate about a problem or concern they have had, past or present. It might be their own experience, or that of a close friend or relation. For example, a difficult decision or relationship, bereavement, unemployment, clash with boss, etc. Give everyone a couple of minutes to reflect and decide. Only one member in each group of four is allowed to "sit out"; their turn will come in the next session! Make it clear that one of the remaining three could talk about a happy, amusing or interesting experience, here in Block 1, but by the time of Block 2, the conversations need to focus on difficulties. If all three "talkers" are ready with a problem, it doesn't matter who goes first, so let someone who feels fairly confident volunteer. They should then speak for about 5 minutes. This first time the others must simply listen. They can only interrupt if they cannot hear or do not understand something the speaker says.

Warn people when they have only 1 minute left. Then stop them and allow at least 10 minutes for de-briefing, i.e.:

(a) For 5 minutes the listeners should talk back to the speaker about the problem, questioning, discussing, advising.

(b) For 5 minutes they should talk over the experience of simply listening – what was easy, difficult, frustrating, rewarding about it? What did they gain or lose from not being allowed to interrupt?

Take general soundings from the full course at this point, on what they have found helpful or difficult. Remind people that listening is not only helpful when we befriend people in some kind of trouble. Every friendship, marriage or group will be enriched if we have become better listeners.

BLOCK 2: RESPONDING

1. You've got to say something!

Quiz 20 mins

Explain that when you are trying to help someone with a problem, you cannot of course just listen and say nothing at all *throughout* the conversation! Give everyone a copy of pages 194–195 from the members' pages which mentions the natural stages of a conversation where we are bound to say something. Working alone or in their core groups, people should decide which they think sounds the best kind of response to make, and why. Stress that, obviously, there is no automatically right or wrong answer; a lot depends on the circumstances and tone of voice; and in some cases we think two alternatives are equally good. But they embody principles that it is good to weigh up.

After 10 minutes, take sample answers from round the groups. Ask people what they like about the options they have chosen, and what they dislike about those they have rejected. For what it's worth, our preferences are:

(a) (i) General, unthreatening opening;

or (iii) Offers the chance to say no to a chat.

(b) (i) Question helping to clarify the meaning for the listener;

or (ii) Feeds back to the speaker what the listener has heard. This is a particularly helpful approach, and may be worth pausing a moment to ask people why. For example, it shows that you have understood what the person is saying and feeling; it encourages them in their train of thought to release more of what is inside; it gives them a chance to try again if they have not expressed what they meant.

(c) (ii) Question helping to see the problem from the other person's point of view.

(d) (ii) A good balance of neither condemning a difficult relationship nor condoning its possible unhelpful outcome.

(e) Depending on the circumstances, any approach might be appropriate; but we prefer:

(i) Questions helping to clarify the problem and pointing to the best source of guidance;

or (ii) Introducing Bible teaching into the discussion, but in a gentle, open-ended way.

(f) (i) Supporting by pinpointing the issues, but leaving the decision where it belongs.

(g)(ii) Leaving door open for further contact, and assuring of support;

or (iii) Suggesting some action to take in the search for a solution.

2. Respond as well as listen

Sharing   25 mins

(a) Ask a second person in each group to prepare to relate a problem or painful experience. One of the others should be the listener, who should *only* respond by checking and questioning (stages b and c on page 194). This listener should take time to think, if need be, before clarifying, feeding back the message he or she is hearing from the speaker, or trying to explore the experience from the inside. The other members of each group are to act as observers.

After 5 minutes ask the observers to comment to the speaker and listener on how the process seemed to be working.

(b) Exchange roles in the groups again. A third member now shares their experience with a different listener and observers. The listener should try to make use of whatever he or she has learnt in this session about listening and responding! This time the conversation can go beyond the checking and questioning stages. After 5 minutes, ask the observers to comment on the listener.

For the final 5 minutes take general comments and questions from the full course. Close with a few moments of silence, when people can pray for their partners in the problems they have shared, and bring to God any pain or doubt that their own problem may have reawakened. Sharing problems can remind some people that they have "unfinished business" to sort out. So offer to be available afterwards to listen to anyone who would like to talk further.

LEADER'S NOTES

SESSION 4

Helping other people: listening and responding

BLOCK 1: LISTENING

■ Watching listening happen

In the demonstration conversation, see if you can spot these things happening:

(A) DISTRESS SIGNALS TO LOOK OUT FOR

(i) Emotional tone of voice.

(ii) The look on the face.

(iii) "Body language" (i.e. gestures, positions, posture).

(iv) Dress and appearance.

(B) GOOD WAYS TO LISTEN

(i) Relax.

(ii) Show you are interested.

(iii) Concentrate.

(iv) Respond non-verbally (nod, smile, genuine sympathetic noises, etc.)

(v) Allow the other person to steer the conversation.

(C) BLOCKS TO LISTENING

(i) Interrupting silences.

(ii) Switching off.

(iii) Shortage of time.

SESSION 4

Helping other people: listening and responding

BLOCK 2: RESPONDING

■ You've got to say something!

Here are seven stages of a conversation with someone who has a problem. In each case tick the phrase which sounds the best kind of thing to say, and be ready to discuss why you chose as you did.

(A) BEGINNING

(i) "How's everything going?"

(ii) "Sorry about your difficulties – I'd love to chat things over with you."

(iii) "Would you like to talk about it or have you got all the help you want?"

(B) CHECKING

(i) "When you say you feel bad about it, do you just mean you feel upset, or actually that you did the wrong thing?"

(ii) "You seem to be saying that you felt really hurt by what she said."

(iii) "I don't understand that."

(C) QUESTIONING

(i) "What do you privately think about what she said?"

(ii) "Why do you think she might have said that?"

(iii) "Don't you think she said that because she's so jealous?"

(D) COMMENTING

(i) "But you shouldn't have a non-Christian boyfriend!"

(ii) "Well no, I don't think would be right to *marry* someone who is not a Christian, but let's look at your relationship with Keith now."

(iii) "It's not my job to comment on the rights and wrongs of the relationship. I'm just trying to help you sort out your misunderstanding with Keith."

(E) USING THE BIBLE

(i) "Would it help to look at the relevant Bibe teaching, or is that not what you're asking?"

(ii) "Do you think this passage has any bearing on the problem?"

(iii) "God makes it perfectly clear in the Bible that ..."

For **Ready to Serve** course use only © Bible Society 1995

(F) SUPPORTING

(i) "It seems to me there are three things you might do; which seems best to you?"

(ii) "I'm sure the best thing for you to do is X."

(iii) "You leave this to me; I'll see her for you."

(G) ENDING

(i) "We can go on talking as long as you like."

(ii) "Do let me know what you decide; I'll be praying for you."

(iii) "Why not ask your friend what it would involve?"

■ Session 5 ■

Outreach: telling people about Jesus

AIM

We move now from helping other people in general to the greatest help a Christian could ever give someone who is not yet a Christian: helping them to become one. We recognize that not every member of your course will have the gift of being an evangelist; but some may. In any case, all Christians are called to be witnesses, ready to explain their Christian hope and faith. We recognize too that many Christians fight shy of the idea of having to talk about their faith on their own. Jesus sent his followers out two-by-two, and there can be great benefit in working together like that; the session gives practice in this partnership evangelism.

BLOCK 1: WHAT WILL YOU SAY?

1. "What exactly would I need to do to become a Christian?"

Role play   5 mins

Announce that the skill practised in this session is the specialized form of listening and responding, when a Christian has the chance to explain their faith to a friend enquiring about it. Take as your motto for the session 1 Peter 3.15–16:

> "Be ready at all times to answer anyone who asks you to explain the hope you have in you, but do it with gentleness and respect."

Ask two in each core group to be themselves, while the others play the part of people very interested in Christianity. They ask how to become a Christian, and must not accept any answer that they would not, in that position, understand. The two "Christians" must respond as they think best.

Stop after 3 minutes and ask people how they are getting on. Encourage them to admit that it is hard work. Ask one or two to give examples of the difficulties they met.

2. What you might say

Discussion   20 mins

On page 199 in the members' pages there is an outline often used in presenting the Good News. Ask

people to mention any others they have used or seen. At the bottom of the page there is space to list pros and cons of using such outlines. Ask people to point out some of the possible disadvantages: mechanical, inflexible, impersonal, possible to forget(!), confusing for the listener to chase all over the Bible, etc. But then ask people to list the positive advantages: helps you understand it yourself, keeps you from getting distracted, confronts people with the Bible, rather than just your ideas, etc. Those who claim that outlines are artificial should ruthlessly be made to be honest about how often they get round to explaining the Good News without one! Suggest that, at least in the early stages of trying to help friends become Christians, it can be a great help to memorize and use an outline as a basis.

3. Another outline of the good news

Discussion   15 mins

Ask people to take a closer look at a carefully worked out outline. Alone or in their groups, they should work through the outline and the Bible passages on pages 199–202. Tell them they are aiming to understand thoroughly what these verses say, and what bearing they have on becoming a Christian, so that they could bring them naturally into a conversation.

Be available to help people with any parts they do not understand.

4. Try an outline

Role play   5 mins

Rotate people in groups so that you have at least one new "enquiring outsider" and one new "Christian". Of the two Christians, one should be a "senior partner", taking the lead in explaining the Good News with the help of a simple outline. This need not be one of the outlines in the members' pages, if they know another one; but at least the ones in the members' pages are there to follow and fall back on. The other Christian should listen prayerfully, and be ready to join in the conversation to help, if the "enquirers" have difficulty understanding or accepting anything.

5. "But people never ask me how to become a Christian"

Short talk   5 mins

A common objection is that the kind of conversation in the role play is unreal and would seldom, if ever, happen. This is your opportunity as leader to make a short challenging exhortation. Unless Christians are willing and ready to press their friends to come to Jesus (also bearing in mind "gentleness and respect"), many will lose out on God's offer of salvation. You could include these points if you feel them to be appropriate.

(A) WHERE ARE YOU GOING?

There is no point even beginning to talk about Jesus if you have no clear idea where

you want to get to in the end. Keep heading towards a clear explanation of how to become a Christian, unless and until you are stopped because your friend has lost interest or has a major obstacle to belief that needs to be dealt with first. We should of course respect this if it appears; but many are more willing to hear what Christianity is about than we assume.

(B) WHERE IS THE INITIATIVE?

In any conversation between two people, each of them will take the initiative and push the chat along into new subjects. On the subject of Christianity you know more than your friend, who will therefore expect you to take the initiative and lead the conversation.

For example, you might try saying, "I think I've said all I can about X for now. Can I go on to Y, which is more the heart of the matter? I think that will help us understand X better, if you want to come back to it later."

(C) WHERE IS YOUR FAITH?

Do you honestly think you're never going to be used to bring someone to Jesus?

Look up Matthew 4.18–20. Jesus is in the business of employing spiritual fishermen who will be given the ability to catch fish. For that you need two pieces of equipment: (i) a grasp of the heart of the Good News, and (ii) simple faith in the living God. If we ask and trust for opportunities, he will give them. Our task is to "be ready at all times" (1 Peter 3.15).

BLOCK 2: WHO, WHEN, WHERE AND HOW?

1. How many of the people you know are not Christians?

List-forming   15 mins

Everyone should begin working alone on page 203 from the members' pages. The aim is to review their friends who are not Christians, and try to discern the one in whom God's Spirit is most clearly at work, leading them towards Jesus. Explain that not all the circles will apply to everyone; obviously, some do not go out to work, or are in education; for some, home and family are in the same place, etc.

For the last 2 to 3 minutes, they should compare notes with the others in their core group.

2. What is the natural next step?

Planning   15 mins

The groups should now help each other talk through the most likely next step towards Christian faith for the particular non-Christian friend they have decided on. They should work through the possible ideas on page 204. When they have

LEADER'S NOTES

decided the right direction to head in, they should plan the practical next step for *them* to take, and write it near the bottom of the page.

Probably they will make different plans for each of their friends; but if they realize they could take joint action, so much the better.

After 10 minutes take soundings from the groups and be ready to move into serious discussion of planning an evangelistic home meeting, service, event, holiday, etc., if a substantial number are asking for this. If the plans sound varied, or if a substantial number are talking of taking an informal initiative themselves, move on to activity (3).

3. What would you say to this friend?

Role play   10 mins

One member of each group should now play the part of their own friend, ideally someone who has not yet been a "non-Christian" in the session. This friend responds positively to the next step you have taken, and wants to talk further about what it means to be a Christian. In the light of everything you have discussed in this session, the others in the group should try to hold the conversation. They, of course, do not know the person so well; but they will have found out a certain amount in activities (1) and (2).

After 5 minutes, they should stop and take stock of what they have learnt through the exercise. What can all of them learn for how they might approach their own friend? On reflection, do people want to modify the "next steps" they were planning? If so, how? Record the detail at the bottom of page 204.

4. Prayer

5 mins

End the session by praying together, either as a full course or in groups, for the people and plans you have been discussing.

SESSION 5

Outreach: telling people about Jesus

BLOCK 1: WHAT WILL YOU SAY?

■ What you might say

AN OUTLINE OF THE GOOD NEWS
Being a true Christian is knowing Jesus Christ – John 17.3.
How can this come about in your life?

(a) Something to ADMIT
That you have gone wrong and so are cut off from God.
Mark 7.14–23 (especially 20–23); Isaiah 59.1–2

(b) Something to BELIEVE
That Jesus brought forgiveness of your sins by dying on the cross.
Romans 5.1–11 (especially 6–11)

(c) Something to CONSIDER
That Jesus must be Lord of your life.
Mark 8.34–35

(d) Something to DO
Commit yourself to following Jesus Christ.
John 1.11–12; Mark 8.34–35

USING OUTLINES TO TELL PEOPLE ABOUT JESUS

DISADVANTAGES	ADVANTAGES
....	....
....	....
....	....
....	....
....	....
....	....

■ Another outline of the good news

A friend of yours is really quite interested in Christianity. You have discussed aspects of it together frequently. Some of the things they have said recently make you think that you should spell out the Good News for them, and show them clearly how to become a Christian.

How will you do it? Following the six steps below is one way. To make *sure* that you know *exactly* what you will say about each of these steps, look up the Bible verses for each and think carefully about how you would explain the ideas they contain. The intermediate questions below are to help you do this. The first Q in each section is a suggested question to ask your friend; the A at the end is the answer that the Bible passage seems to us to provide.

(1) **Q. WHAT'S AT THE HEART OF BEING A CHRISTIAN?**
Look up John 17.3.
By "eternal life", Jesus didn't just mean living for ever, or life after death; he meant ....

It is a *quality* of life that can start ....

A. KNOWING THE LORD JESUS PERSONALLY.

(2) **Q. WHAT'S STOPPING YOU FROM KNOWING THE LORD JESUS NOW?**
Look up Mark 7.20–23.
This picture of what all people are really like shows that God isn't just

concerned about our outward actions, but about our ....

....

Even if we haven't actually *done* all these things, we may well have thought them. How seriously does God regard our thoughts (see Matthew 5.21–22,

27–28)? ....

....

A. THERE ARE WRONG THINGS IN YOUR LIFE.

(3) **Q. WHY DOES THAT STOP YOU FROM KNOWING THE LORD JESUS?**
Look up Isaiah 59.1–2.
You may ask, "So what? I'm not perfect, but does it really matter all that

much?" Isaiah says that it *does* matter, because our sins ....

....

"Sin" is another word for all the wrong things Jesus listed in Mark 7 and Matthew 5. That is why God seems distant and unreal. It's like the weather on a cloudy day: there's not so much light or warmth, but that's not because the sun isn't there any more. It's there all right, but it isn't shining through to us because of the clouds.

A. IT MAKES A BARRIER BETWEEN YOU AND GOD.

(4) Q. HOW CAN THAT BARRIER BE REMOVED?

Look up Isaiah 53.6.

This is a remarkable prophecy of what would happen to God's Servant, Jesus Christ, and why. Write out the part of this verse that tells us the

same truth as we saw in Mark 7 and Matthew 5: ....

....

According to this verse, when Jesus was suffering and dying, what did God do with all our sin?

....

Sin *always* cuts a person off from God, even when that person was God's own Son. Look up Matthew 27.46. What tells you in that verse that this separation really happened?

....

....

Sin was making a separation between Jesus and God; only it wasn't *his* sin, it was ours.

A. JESUS TOOK IT ON HIMSELF ON THE CROSS.

(5) Q. SO IS THERE ANYTHING LEFT FOR YOU TO DO?

Look up Mark 8.34–35.

Jesus said that if we want to become his followers, we must ....
ourselves. This means, instead of running our own lives, doing what *we*
want with our time, money, friendships, abilities, we will hand over control
of those things to .... We are not perfect, and often *in fact*
we will not let the Lord have this place of top priority in our lives. But we
must decide *at heart* that we want to do so, at the outset of our lives as
Christians.

To "carry your cross" means being prepared to .... your life in
the service of God.

A. HAND OVER CONTROL OF YOUR LIFE TO JESUS.

(6) Q. EXACTLY HOW DO YOU DO THIS?

Look up Mark 1.14–18.

Jesus gives two commands in verse 15:

(a) Repent (NIV) or turn away from your sins (GNB). We need to agree with
    Jesus that they are wrong, and accept his help to give them up. This is
    probably best done by praying to him silently.

(b) .... the good news. We may not *feel* forgiven, but he tells
    us we are. We need to take him at his word.

    Then Jesus gives a third command to Simon and Andrew in verse 17:

(c) .... me. This is just as possible in the twentieth century as it was in the first. We trust him to be with us through the Holy Spirit; we learn what his instructions for living are in the Bible and we follow them.

A.   REPENT, BELIEVE AND FOLLOW JESUS CHRIST.

If, at the end of your conversation, your friend is still not really sure about becoming a Christian, what else might you do, say or suggest?

....

....

....

Outreach: telling people about Jesus

BLOCK 2: WHO, WHEN, WHERE AND HOW?

■ How many of the people you know are not Christians?

List any people you know who are not Christians, in whichever of the spheres of your life they belong to:

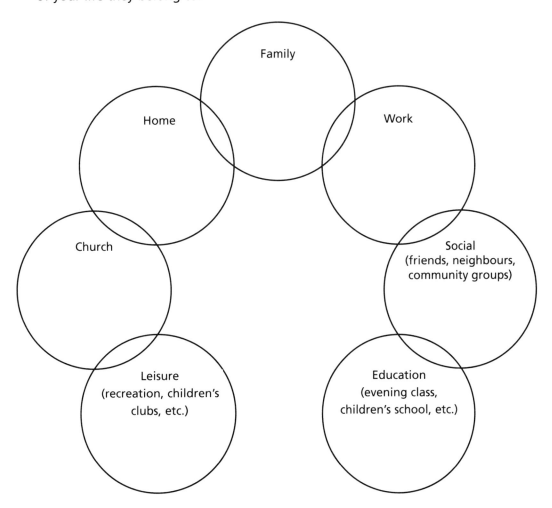

Now choose the one who seems to you most likely to be interested in

becoming a Christian: ....

Adapted from *Church Growth II* a Bible Society training course handbook.

■ What is the natural next step?

Do any of the ideas below sound a natural, likely way for your friend to move closer to Christian commitment? Don't worry if a particular form of event does not appear to be happening in your area; it could be arranged. Tick any ideas that sound worth exploring. If none of them do, try to think of your own, better ideas.

(a) Invite them to an informal meal or social event, to get to know each other better, and to introduce other Christian friends to them.

(b) Invite them to an evangelistic home meeting or discussion group.

(c) Invite them to an evangelistic service (*whether or not your church has planned one in the immediate future*).

(d) Invite them to a big local evangelistic event.

(e) Invite them to a Christian concert, entertainment, or film.

(f) Invite them to a Christian holiday or conference.

(g) Lend them a Christian book, magazine, tape or video.

(h) Ask them directly if you could explain to them how to become a Christian.

(i) (other) ....

(j) (other) ....

What is the next practical move for *you* to make, towards this plan to help your friend get nearer to becoming a Christian? (For example, is there something you need to find out? Someone to consult? Or is the first thing to make time to pray? If so, *when* and *what* for?)

....

....

....

Any extra ideas at the end of the session?

....

....

For **Ready to Serve** course use only © Bible Society 1995

■ Session 6 ■

Speaking in public

AIM

This session does not touch on preaching or giving talks – for these, see "Where to find further training" on page 222. "Speaking in public" at this stage covers the occasions when we need to stand up and read or say something aloud in a service: announcements, reading the Bible, prayers, introducing songs, reports, sharing experiences and using drama.

BLOCK 1: MAKING ANNOUNCEMENTS

1. Chairman Muddlehead

Monologue drama 10 mins

In advance give a copy of the script on page 207 to a confident actor or reader, and tell them to be prepared to perform the sketch now. It will be best if the words are written down on separate scraps of paper, or cut-up photocopies. The character in question is male, so you may prefer to use a male "actor".

Ask everyone else to observe and comment on the ways in which it demonstrates how *not* to make announcements.

2. Stand and deliver

Practical workshop 30 mins

The task for everyone is described on members' pages 208–209. How you structure it will depend on your numbers and the space at your disposal. The

ideal arrangement is to combine two of the core groups in a room or open space, where they will not disturb other groups. Allocate one announcement from the list to each person, and give them 5 minutes to prepare it. Have scrap paper available.

Before people start making their announcements, ask everyone to look at the check-list of qualities to be watching in each speaker. After each announcement, the listeners should comment briefly and constructively on how well the announcer "scored" on the qualities in the check-list.

3. And now Jane has got the notices . . .

Check-list 5 mins

As a summary of the skills discussed in this block, ask people to read and reflect on the instructions on page 209.

BLOCK 2: GIVING A LEAD IN SERVICES

1. Helping to lead in services

Buzz-groups 15 mins

People should work in their core groups. Assign *one* of the areas of service-leading detailed on pages 210–211 to each group. Only cover areas which are relevant to your church.

2. Report or prepare

15 mins

Two from each group (or one from a threesome) should contribute to a central pooling of ideas. They should report their group's list of instructions, and make notes of other groups' lists. One of them or an assistant leader should record all the ideas on a board or OHP, if it helps. During or after this session, or at the beginning of the next (or between the two!), pass on all this wisdom to the people who are not in this central pool, perhaps in the form of a typed copy.

Meanwhile, the other two in each group should prepare an item for a time of fellowship and prayer together, to take place at the end of this block. They should work on something in the area their group has discussed, and according to the instructions they have drawn up.

They may decide that only one of them will speak out loud, in which case the other helps in preparation (for example, helps choose a reading from the Bible, and then listens to a practice to comment on how easy the reader is to hear, follow, understand, etc.). Or they may decide they could both speak in public (for example, one interviewing the other on a recent experience).

Circulate round these groups as they prepare. Co-ordinate their contributions to this closing time of ministering to each other and the Lord. Provide musical accompaniment for any songs, if possible. Decide what order to take the various ingredients in.

3. Serve each other and the Lord

Short service   15 mins

Now simply ask each person or pair to step forward and lead. Administer "first aid" if necessary, but do not comment on people's contributions in public. Allow it to be a genuine time of "ministry", serving each other in Jesus' name.

Chairman Muddlehead

This is a monologue showing how not to make announcements. Muddlehead is the chair of a meeting, or the notice-giver in a church service. The notices given are written on various bits of paper – one on an old envelope, another on the back of a card, etc. They are in the wrong order, and some are the wrong way up, wrong way round, etc. The effect, as they are given out and then the bits of paper put down on the table or lectern, is rather like a game of snap. When not actually hunting through the pack or reading from the page, he looks at the ceiling or at the walls – anywhere but at the listeners' faces. The voice should be monotonous and totally lacking in interest.

MUDDLEHEAD: And now for this week's notices.

Your women's Tuesday meeting will be next Friday, owing to the renovations at the church; but the following week it will be on Wednesday, so that will be much easier to remember. We trust that we shall revert to the normal meeting time on Thursdays in the not-too-distant future.

On Saturday the young people will be having their church supper. Last month, I understand, it was a great success; and they are all asked to bring the same food as before.

And now we are very sorry to have to say goodbye to our treasurer, Mr Lucre. As you know, he and his family are going down to live in Bournemouth. This is a great loss to us all. Mr Lucre was born here and brought up here, and we hoped that he would have died here, but this is not to be. We wish the Lucres journeying mercies.

And now it is a great privilege and pleasure to have as our missionary speaker Dr Phyllis Murphy. We had hoped it would have been Dr George Bashem, but he was unable to come, and, after all, Dr Murphy is a doctor, even though a lady, and we are very glad that she has managed to come all the way from ...from ... er ... where have you come from, dear sister? Ah yes, you are living just down the road while on furlough. We trust that the Lord will be blessing you through this time of being laid aside, and that you will be learning something from us in this corner of his vineyard. So we must listen to Dr Murphy patiently, and we shall be able to have Dr Bashem another time.

SESSION 6

Speaking in public

BLOCK 1: MAKING ANNOUNCEMENTS

■ Stand and deliver

Imagine that you are responsible for one of the "notices" or announcements in your church service. You have 5 minutes to work out further details for one of the following announcements, prepare the wording, and be ready to make the announcement as if for real. The others will comment on how you came over.

(a) Advance notice of a wedding.

(b) Last week's offerings.

(c) Welcome and introduce visiting preacher.

(d) Announce this week's Bible study and prayer meeting.

(e) Arrangements for a "love-gift" for your minister, who is away this Sunday.

(f) News of a church member who is critically ill, in need of prayer.

(g) Plans for the church day outing.

(h) Explain and introduce a moment in the service when members greet each other informally; in some churches this is called the Peace.

(i) Church hymn-books and orders of service have been disappearing – inadvertently, you are sure! A gentle reproach to members for being absent-minded or careless, and for the inconvenience they have caused.

(j) News of one of your members who is a missionary overseas.

Qualities to be watching in each speaker

(a) Mastery: the announcer knows what he or she is talking about.

(b) Relevance: sticking to the point.

(c) Brevity: keeping things as short as possible, but with nothing important left out.

(d) Awareness of listeners' point of view.

(e) Easy to understand.

(f) Interesting to listen to.

(g) Sense of what is fitting for the occasion and the subject.

(h) Humour (if fitting).

(i) "Getting through" to listeners.

(j) Easy to remember.

(k) Easy to hear.

(l) Appearance: suitable for the subject and mood of the announcement?

(m) Gestures: helpful or distracting?

■ And now Jane has got the notices . . .

Stand up . . . unless you are over 5 feet tall when seated.

Breathe in . . . hard. Filled lungs help to settle restless nerves.

Speak up . . . few voices are powerful enough to fill a large room when speaking at their normal level.

Look up . . . this helps your voice to travel further.

Open up . . . your mouth. Well, of course. Not everybody does, though!

Look at . . . your listeners. Eye to eye contact can be very powerful.

Write out . . . what you are going to say – until you are experienced enough to manage without.

Space out . . . your words, not swallowing them, spitting, stumbling over them, or spluttering.

Shut up . . . as soon as you've finished. Don't waffle on and on and on and on and on!

Written by Sybil Green for "Inter-School" magazine No. 9, 1976. Published by Scripture Union.

Speaking in public

BLOCK 2: GIVING A LEAD IN SERVICES

■ Helping to lead in services

Take *one* of these parts of a service. List as many tips or hints as you can think of to guide someone doing the task for the first time, and wanting it to be as effective as possible. It doesn't matter how small or how obvious you think the instructions are; write them all down.

(a) Reading the Bible

....

....

....

....

....

(b) Leading prayers

....

....

....

....

....

(c) Introducing hymns, psalms, or choruses for everyone to sing

....

....

....

....

....

For **Ready to Serve** course use only © Bible Society 1995

(d) Giving a brief report of an inter-church meeting, which you attended as the church's representative

....

....

....

....

....

(e) Sharing good news from your own recent spiritual experience (for example, how you become a Christian, an answer to prayer, etc.)

....

....

....

....

....

(f) Using drama

....

....

....

....

....

■ Session 7 ■

What job *does* God want me to do in my church?

AIM

It is vital to take stock at the end of a practical course like this. What have your course members discovered? What help do they need next? This series has only covered the first steps in Christian ministry, giving people a sample of what is involved in being an active church member. In no sense has it given an adequate training for the job God wants each of them to do. You should help people see what further training they need, and where they might be able to find it.

But before they make future plans in Block 2, we feel it is vital that they establish an atmosphere of security through the opening celebration and the expressions of appreciation in Block 1.

BLOCK 1: THANKS ALL ROUND

1. Celebration

10 mins

Plan to set a festive mood by starting with some singing and praise, and some encouraging words from the Bible. If your course members are doing the home assignments, ask one of the core groups to open this session with the act of celebration they have prepared.

2. Heavenly harmony?

Sharing

10 mins

In their groups, people should fill in the fun survey on pages 214–215 of the members' pages. It is a gentle way of showing how they appreciate the contribution that each member has made to their group, and leads into the more thorough "strength bombardment" of the next activity.

3. Strength bombardment

Sharing

25 mins

This is an extremely positive exercise and should not be rushed. Provide a sheet of rough paper and a smaller slip of paper for each person, and a hat or small box for each group.

Everyone starts by listing on their sheet of paper what they see as the strong points and good qualities in the personalities and abilities of the other group members. Weak points or defects do not enter this exercise at all! Everyone should *keep hold of their own sheet*.

On the smaller slip, people anonymously write what they see as their own strengths. They should then fold these slips, put them into the hat or box, and mix them up.

The first person draws out a slip and reads out the list of strengths, whether or not it is their own paper. The others guess who wrote it, and the writer owns up to it when they guess correctly. From the first list of everyone's strong points, which they have retained, the others say what further strengths they discern in the writer, beyond what he or she has seen in her or himself. If he or she does not know how to respond, they should simply say thank you.

When this has finished, the second person draws a slip of paper, and so on.

BLOCK 2: WHAT IT ALL ADDS UP TO

1. Am I doing the right job in my church?

Questionnaire   30 mins

Work on pages 216–218 from the members' pages. The exercise is designed to help people check the direction in which their abilities qualify them to serve Jesus Christ and his church. Everyone should complete the survey for themselves and then compare their findings with the rest of their core group. The others are there to agree with or question each person's self-assessment; and to support and advise those whose findings come as a surprise!

Ask them to spend the last 5 minutes discussing the two questions on page 218.

2. Where do I go from here?

Reflection   15 mins

If learning and growing are really to take place, it is vital to take stock here of what God has taught each person through this session and series, and what he wants them to do about it. Page 219 gives space for these conclusions and resolutions. Members of the core groups should help each other fill them in.

Close with a few moments of silence for people to turn their thoughts into prayer. Then lead in a final, spoken prayer yourself. Announce that you are available to talk to anyone who wants to discuss what they should do next.

As well as any initiatives of their own that course members want to take, you may well have formed your own ideas about what would make a helpful follow-on to *Ready to Serve*. In particular, if people are going to take on new responsibilities in church life (or even continue with old ones), they need more thorough training than *Ready to Serve* can provide. They should receive this within the next year. You will find suggestions on where to find further training in the next section. If you have already made plans or would rather float some ideas for discussion, announce them now.

LEADER'S NOTES

What job *does* God want me to do in my church?

BLOCK 1: THANKS ALL ROUND

■ Heavenly harmony?

This is a light-hearted way to show how you appreciate the contribution made to your group by the other members. Think of your group as a band: which instrument below reminds you of each member in your group's music? If none of them fits, add a better suggestion below. When you have finished, compare notes with the rest of the group.

GROUP MEMBER	INSTRUMENT
....	*Angel's harp*: soft, gentle, tuneful; "heavenly music".
....	*Pub piano*: mischievous, raucous, honky-tonk; delightfully carefree.
....	*Kettle drum*: strong and commanding when needed, but usually in the background.
....	*Spanish castanets*: wild and exotic, but able to lead the dance.
....	*Leading violin*: wide-ranging, clear-thinking, calling the tune – with the touch of the maestro.
....	*Fluttering flute*: independent, high-soaring, and clear as crystal.
....	*Scottish bagpipes*: growling, grating, military – but gets things moving.
....	*Magical oboe*: thoughtful, haunting, peace-making – a real snake-charmer!
....	*Mellow cello*: warm, harmonious, compassionate – adding body and depth to the music.
....	*Cathedral organ*: inspiring, uplifting, versatile – everything on the grand scale.

....   *Trumpet fanfare*: commanding and lively, signalling attention and attack.

....   *One-man band*: mouth organ, accordion, cymbals and drum – the complete solo entertainer.

....   *Comb and tissue-paper*: home-made, creative, uncomplicated, childlike and fun.

....   *Acoustic guitar*: informal, ideal accompaniment to everyone else's singing.

....   *Other*:

SESSION 7

What job *does* God want me to do in my church?

BLOCK 2: WHAT IT ALL ADDS UP TO

■ Am I doing the right job in my church?

A spiritual job-finder

Read the following statements and mark yourself out of 5 for each. If you give yourself 5 it will be one of your very strong points. If you give yourself O or 1 it will be one of your very weak points.

MARK

....   (1) I am good at listening.

....   (2) I enjoy explaining things to others from the Bible.

....   (3) I am quite gifted musically.

....   (4) I am often used to help others become Christians.

....   (5) People often ask me to do the practical organizing and planning.

....   (6) I feel a deep, caring love for those who are ill, and want to help them get well.

....   (7) I like making or designing things.

....   (8) I am deeply concerned about world problems and people in need.

....   (9) I am usually looked to for a lead.

....   (10) I make helpful relationships with others easily.

....   (11) Others say they are helped when I teach them things about Jesus and Christian living.

....   (12) I have a feel for words, and enjoy reading, both alone and aloud.

....   (13) God has given me a great love for others and a longing to put them in touch with him.

....   (14) I can organize well, clearly and efficiently.

....   (15) Others find my presence soothing and healing.

.... (16) I like helping other people.

.... (17) I am active in service in the community.

.... (18) In a group I am often elected chairman or leader.

.... (19) Others seem to find me encouraging, and share their problems with me.

.... (20) I love study and finding the facts.

.... (21) People say they like my drawings, designs, other artwork.

.... (22) I find my life is full of opportunities to witness to Jesus Christ.

.... (23) I enjoy office work and do it thoroughly.

.... (24) I have sometimes given advice to the sick and they have been helped.

.... (25) I am a practical type, good at do-it-yourself jobs and making use of odds and ends.

.... (26) I am very aware of people who are deprived today, and feel I should do something about them.

.... (27) When leading something I get deeply interested and put a lot of work into it.

.... (28) I really care about other people.

.... (29) I am patient when helping others understand about Christianity; it seems so worthwhile.

.... (30) I have a deep desire to express myself and my faith in creative, artistic ways.

.... (31) I love to talk to others about Jesus.

.... (32) I am painstaking about details in organization.

.... (33) I spend time praying with and for sick people.

.... (34) I spend a lot of time helping others in practical ways.

.... (35) Social and political issues seem to me to be crying out for Christian witness and involvement.

.... (36) I am good at sharing work with others in a team.

Now fill in the mark you gave yourself alongside each point number below:

(1)	(10)	(19)	(28)	A total: ....
(2)	(11)	(20)	(29)	B total: ....
(3)	(12)	(21)	(30)	C total: ....
(4)	(13)	(22)	(31)	D total: ....
(5)	(14)	(23)	(32)	E total: ....
(6)	(15)	(24)	(33)	F total: ....
(7)	(16)	(25)	(34)	G total: ....
(8)	(17)	(26)	(35)	H total: ....
(9)	(18)	(27)	(36)	I total: ....

Add up the totals along each line and place them at the end of the column.
If your highest total is in column:

A   your gifts lie in a pastoral direction

B   teaching

C   artistic

D   evangelistic

E   administrative

F   healing

G   practical help

H   service to society

I   leadership

Adapted from a survey compiled by Lewis Misselbrook, reprinted on pages 452-3 of *I Believe in Church Growth*, © 1981 Eddie Gibbs published by Hodder and Stoughton Ltd.

Two questions to discuss

(a) Am I doing the right job in my church?

(b) Should I be doing something else instead or as well?

■ Where do I go from here?

(a) Through this session, God has shown me that:

....

....

....

....

....

(b) Through this series, God has shown me that:
(Flip back through your worksheets to remind yourself of recent sessions. In particular, were there areas of Christian service where you felt you had something to offer?)

....

....

....

....

....

(c) As a result, I now need to:

....

....

....

....

....

(d) The person or people I should talk to about this is or are:

....

....

(e) My next immediate step will be to:

....

....

Something to do at home

We strongly recommend that you do some further work at home between sessions of this series. This will help you go on thinking about the course, and begin to put what you are learning into practice.

After session No. 1

BIBLE STUDY

(a) (optional) Compare the last time you led a group Bible study with the "Five tips for the group leader" on pages 166–167.

(b) (optional) If you did not look in the session at the programme for preparing a Bible study on pages 167–168, do so now. Follow its instructions and suggested timings to prepare a group study outline on a short favourite passage of yours. If you're not sure what any of the instructions mean, look at the sample outline on pages 167–168.

(c) (optional) Look up Mark 10.35–45. What can we learn from Jesus' example and teaching here about the way we should lead group Bible study? (Obviously, the passage is not *about* leading Bible study, but notice what Jesus says about a Christian leader's motives and ambitions; and his own way of answering questions.)

(d) (recommended) Prepare to lead a full group Bible study. *Either*, if you belong to a regular Bible study group, the passage set for the next time you meet, *whether or not* you will in fact be leading it; *or* Luke 11.1–13, adapting pages 167–168 to make a suitable outline for yourself. Write section titles, general questions, further questions and introduction. Be ready to lead your core group in an extract from this in the next session.

After session No. 2

PRAYER TIME

(a) Arrange to lead a prayer time in your church or fellowship group, as soon as possible. Write notes to guide you. Apply the ideas and suggestions from this session. Finish working through pages 174–181 if you did not do so at the time.

or (and)

(b) Write a short report of the next prayer time you attend, commenting on the ways you think it was helpfully led, and the ways in which it could have been even better. If at all possible, discuss your report with the leader of the prayer time.

After session No. 3

UNDERSTANDING

Write down the name of someone you know well, who has problems at the moment. It could be the person you thought about at the end of the session; but it would be better practice for you to start again with somebody else. Reflect on what you know about the person's background and self-image. Does this help you to understand their problems better? Does it help you see your way more clearly to any advice you could give them? Write a report on what you understand to be the person's needs (keeping the name confidential) to share with your core group.

After session No. 4

LISTENING AND RESPONDING

Continue thinking of your friend with problems. If they are open to talk about their situation with you, make a definite plan to visit them or ring them up in the coming week, at a moment when they will be free to tell you how they feel. Sensitively try to put into practice what you learnt in this session about   listening and responding. If it is natural, and only if everyone concerned is happy with the situation, it might be better for two of you to work together. You can share the responsibility, one of you praying and observing, while the other concentrates on listening and responding. However, it must be stressed how sensitively this must all be done, with a genuine concern for the person involved, rather than just a desire to "try out" what you have learnt. Write a report on how you get on.

After session No. 5

TELLING PEOPLE ABOUT JESUS

Press ahead with the plans you have made for outreach during this session. Obviously they may not occur between sessions 5 and 6, which may be all to the good as it will give you more time to prepare. The next session in this series continues to build up skills which will be helpful in outreach. Write a report on your progress.

After session No. 6

SPEAKING IN PUBLIC

Arrange to meet with your core group. Plan a ten-minute time of celebration to open Session 7, praising God and listening to him. Share the responsibilities between you, and write a master-script. Make sure you include a song or two and a Bible reading. Whatever other ingredients you include, follow the instructions compiled during the session on how to lead or introduce them. (Check that you have got a record of the instructions prepared by the other core groups.) Only one of the groups will, in fact, get the chance to lead the celebration, so think of other occasions when you could put your plans into practice.

Where to find further training

There is an address list of the publishers and training agencies mentioned below on page 223. Ring or write to them for further details.

(A) OTHER TRAINING COURSES IN PRINT

Leading a group meeting

A Health Guide for Small Groups; a training manual for those who lead or belong to small groups, published by Small Group Resources.

Leading small groups; a do-it-yourself training pack, from Scripture Union Training Unit.

Using the Bible; a do-it-yourself training pack, from Scripture Union Training Unit.

Helping other people

Christian Caring; a do-it-yourself training pack, from Scripture Union Training Unit.

Outreach

Come Back Evangelism; a group workbook, from CPAS.

"Good News Down the Street" course; a visiting programme and cassette, from CPAS.

Lights That Shine; a practical workbook, from CPAS.

Sharing Your Faith; a do-it-yourself training pack, from Scripture Union Training Unit.

Two Ways to Live; an evangelistic outline, training course, and audio/video cassette back-up, from St Matthias Press.

Speaking in public

How to Preach or Give Talks; a programmed learning manual, available from SEAN.

Speaking From the Front; a sixty-minute audio cassette on how to plan, deliver and evaluate a talk, by Wendy Palmer.

(B) FACE-TO-FACE TRAINING

The following agencies run public training events or are available to come to your church to lead a training course for you.

Leading a group meeting
CPAS

Scripture Union Training Unit

Small Group Resources

Helping other people

CWR (Crusade for World Revival)

Scripture Union Training Unit

Outreach

CPAS

Speaking in public

Freelance Wordwright (Lance Pierson)

The Proclamation Trust

ADDRESSES AND TELEPHONE NUMBERS OF PUBLISHERS AND TRAINING AGENCIES MENTIONED

Bible Society

Stonehill Green, Westlea, Swindon SN5 7DG ☎ 01793 418100

CPAS (Church Pastoral Aid Society)

Athena Drive, Tachbrook Park, Warwick CV34 6NG ☎ 01926 334242

CWR (Crusade for World Revival)

Waverley Abbey House, Waverley Lane, Farnham GU9 8EP ☎ 01251 83761

Freelance Wordwright (Lance Pierson)

48 Peterborough Road, London SW6 3EB ☎ 0171–731 6544

The Proclamation Trust

5th Floor, B Wing, Plantation House, 31–35 Fenchurch Street, London, EC3M 3DX
☎ 0171–283 2810

St Matthias Press

PO Box 665, London SW20 8RU ☎ 0181–947 5686

Scripture Union Training Unit

26–30 Heathcote Street, Nottingham NG1 3AA ☎ 01159 418144

SEAN (Study by Extension to All Nations) UK

The Pound, Whitestone, Exeter EX4 2HP ☎ 01647 61134

Small Group Resources

1 Hilton Place, Harehills, Leeds L58 4HE ☎ 01132 374974

Wendy Palmer

22 Duffield Court, Chapel Street, Duffield, Belper DE56 4EQ